END

Tragedy to Truth is a MUST read. It is a pure testimony of redemption and healing.

— *Joel Engle*
Pastor of Preaching & Vision, Change Point, Anchorage AK

Without a doubt the most convincing endorsement I can give to Casey's book comes from seeing the impact Casey's story has had on the students in our church, including my own daughter! Casey has been with us on several occasions, and is without a doubt, our students "speaker of choice." Not only is Casey's story incredibly compelling, but also, as a preacher, father, and leader, he lives out the claims his transforming story makes!

—*Victor Flores*
Pastor of Student Ministries, Bell Shoals Baptist Church, Brandon, FL

By far, one of the most compelling redemption stories I have heard in 30 years of ministry. Casey Cease is the real deal, a young man who has been to hell and back with a testimony of God's grace, mercy and forgiveness that even the most cynical among us dare not ignore. Character, depth and genuine spirituality always come to mind when I think of this young pastor and the ministry God has given him over this past decade. How thankful and thrilled I am that his story will finally reach a larger audience.

— *Bob Swan*
Director of Student Ministries The Woodlands Methodist Church, The Woodlands, TX

"Casey Cease has been transformed by the gospel of Jesus Christ! I praise God for His severe mercy on Casey and I believe as you read his story, you will too."

— *Chuck Land*
*Lead Pastor, Crossbridge Church, Sugar Land, TX*

My friend and fellow church-planter, Casey Cease, has written this book about one thing. It's not about bad things happening to good people. It's not about making lemonade out of lemons. Casey's story is about sinful, messed up people being redeemed by the grace of God. Tragedy to Truth is about the gospel of Jesus Christ.

If we could only see the depth of the pain, sin, and confusion that so many people hide in the basements of their souls, we would be shocked. Many of these people even populate our churches on Sunday mornings, afraid of being found out. Casey is offering a glimpse into the mind and heart of someone who spent years searching for fulfillment and coming up empty until his life came to a screeching halt, literally. But his story doesn't end there, because Jesus loves to heal lives that seem broken beyond repair.

The magnitude of the grace and forgiveness available to us in Christ is scandalous to the self-righteous but hopeful for those of us who know we are broken. If you are afraid you have gone too far, sinned too much, and hurt too many people for Jesus to save you, read this book and believe the gospel of Jesus.

— *Patrick Rowe*
*Lead Pastor, Genesis Church, Spring, TX*

In life our Christian faith is often tested. In this book, Casey Cease honestly and clearly tells the story of how he walked through a dreadful trial in his personal faith, and how God used it to enrich Casey's understanding of the Lord's amazing love and grace. You will treasure Tragedy to Truth, and after reading it, you will more gladly sing, "Jesus loves me, this I know."

— *Jason Mirikitani*
*Author, Speaker Mile Marker 825,*
*www.MileMarkerBook.com*

Casey has a story that no one wants to go through but everyone can learn from. The story begins with man's bad decisions and ends with God's redeeming grace. I encourage you to take a good listen and allow God to speak to your heart. You'll be both encouraged and challenged to live your life with greater devotion to Jesus. Casey has been changed by the love of Jesus, let him lead you to the same.

—*Gregg Matte*
*Senior Pastor, Houston's First Baptist Church, Houston, TX*

# TRAGEDY TO TRUTH

# TRAGEDY TO TRUTH

A STORY OF FAITH AND TRANSFORMATION

BY

## CASEY CEASE

WITH
CAROL JONES

LUCIDBOOKS

Tragedy To Truth
Copyright © 2014 by Casey Cease

Published by Lucid Books in Houston, TX.
www.LucidBooks.net

Art Direction & Cover Design: *Zach McNair*

Unless otherwise indicated, Scripture quotations are from the ESV® Bible
(The Holy Bible, English Standard Version®), copyright © 2001 by Crossway.
Used by permission. All rights reserved.

ISBN-10: 1632960095
ISBN-13: 978-1-63296-009-2

Special Sales: Most Lucid Books titles are available in special quantity discounts.
Custom imprinting or excerpting can also be done to fit special needs. Contact
Lucid Books at info@lucidbooks.net.

*Dedicated to my best friend, my beloved, my Steph.*

# CONTENTS

ENDORSEMENTS. . . . . . . . . . . . . . . . . . . . i

FOREWORD . . . . . . . . . . . . . . . . . . . . xiii

PART ONE . . . . . . . . . . . . . . . . . . . . xv

    Chapter 1    The Crash . . . . . . . . . . . . . .1

    Chapter 2    Beginnings . . . . . . . . . . . . . .5

    Chapter 3    Early Years . . . . . . . . . . . . . .9

    Chapter 4    People Pleasers of the World, Please Stand Up . 13

    Chapter 5    Fitting In . . . . . . . . . . . . . . 21

    Chapter 6    Galveston – The Calm Before the Storm . . . 39

    Chapter 7    Self-Destructing . . . . . . . . . . . 43

    Chapter 8    Recovery . . . . . . . . . . . . . . 53

    Chapter 9    The Gradual Decline . . . . . . . . . . 61

    Chapter 10    Conversion . . . . . . . . . . . . . 69

PART TWO . . . . . . . . . . . . . . . . . . . . 75

    Chapter 11    Consequences. . . . . . . . . . . . . 77

    Chapter 12    Anxiety and Depression . . . . . . . . . 83

    Chapter 13    A Field of Broken Wells . . . . . . . . 97

    Chapter 14    Girls . . . . . . . . . . . . . . . 105

    Chapter 15    Temptation . . . . . . . . . . . . . 113

    Chapter 16    Hopeful. . . . . . . . . . . . . . . 123

APPENDIX A–What's Your Story? . . . . . . . . . . . .131

ACKNOWLEDGEMENTS . . . . . . . . . . . . . . . .135

ABOUT THE AUTHOR . . . . . . . . . . . . . . . . .139

# FOREWORD

I have a horrible memory. I can hardly remember what I did yesterday, but despite the fact that July 5th, 1995, was a typical day for me, it is burned with odd vividness in my brain and in my heart. I was 15 years old, and I was walking around our street with a dear, childhood friend.

That evening, rumors of a tragic accident involving two upperclassmen in my high school were spreading: Casey Cease was speeding through his neighborhood and hit and killed his friend, John Kimtantas. Casey had been drinking. I didn't know John at all, and I had met Casey only once. We were barely acquaintances, and as heartbreaking as these kinds of stories always are, this one hit me differently. My heart grieved for Casey, and I couldn't get him out of my mind. I didn't understand why this particular story was haunting me. Little did I know that the Lord was going to connect my life to this date, this horrible event, and this young man forever.

Just a few short months after the accident, a 17-year-old Casey with a tarnished criminal record and a 15-year-old me, the daughter of a police officer, started dating.

Now, when we look back, we realize that it was probably unwise to be in such a serious relationship during such a serious time, but I can't help but be grateful because I witnessed first hand the very power of God! I watched day by day, little by little, our Great and Mighty God transform a boy into a man Someone lost into someone found, and not only found but blessed with purpose and passion and a great resolve to use his story, tragic as it may be, to proclaim the Great Story of Jesus.

Casey and I have been married 12 years now at the writing of this foreword, (we've been together 17 years in all) and I have learned so much about the Lord through His work in Casey. How patient our God is! How endless are His stories of mercy and grace! Molding a heart to look more like Christ's is slow business, but the Lord is steadfast and faithful to the task. I've learned that, more than likely, transformation requires a pit of fire, a den of lions, a season in the desert, but what unfathomable joy there is in knowing Jesus all the more. I have seen God do this work. I have seen Casey face trial after trial. I have seen Casey humbled and broken and humbled again, and I have seen God raise up a better man than before.

With all the people whom Casey knows, I'm certain that there would have been someone better to write this foreword.But I am honored for the opportunity to share with you, perhaps in a way that no one else could, that he is the real deal. He loves Jesus whole-heartedly and desires to live his life as a "thank-you" to the God who saved him and made him new. He loves his family well. I can say with all confidence and sincerity that he tries daily to lay down his life for me as Christ laid His life down for the church. He is a wonderful father who is gracious and patient and ferociously protective of his two beautiful girls. He loves his church and does not take lightly the responsibility he bares in shepherding God's people. He is prayerful and studious and selfless and is desperate for those who are far from God to be reconciled to Him.

As you read, you will see for yourself that Casey is not perfect by any means, he has made many mistakes, some that cannot be undone. Some lessons that he has learned, he has had to repent and relearn again. But he does not mind me saying so, and in fact shares his sin openly with you, so that you might know the depth of God's love for even the most undeserving. No matter how great our sin, God is infinitely greater. No matter how bleak the darkness, Christ can bring a light and a hope.

**Stephanie Cease**
*http://stephcease.blogspot.com*

## PART I
# THE TRAGEDY

CHAPTER 1

# THE CRASH

I woke up covered in glass, a deployed airbag lying lifeless in my lap. Looking up I could barely see through the smoke and the thick cloud of fiberglass in the air. As the fog cleared, I was able to make out a huge hole in my windshield. There was a sharp metallic smell mixed with the pungent odor from my car's fluids. What just happened? I looked down and saw that I was covered with glass and my own blood. Panic rushed over me as I looked around confused. Suddenly, a friend was prying open my passenger side door. I remembered what had just happened and began to panic. "WHO DID I HIT?!"

My friend, Blake, opened my car door as he tried to calm me down. "Can you move your feet?" he asked. Blake was a few years older than I wa s and someone I had always looked up to. He and I were in the theater department at school for his senior year, and both worked as lifeguards. "You didn't hit anyone, just some trees," he said.

He told me that he needed to get me out of the car. There was a lot of smoke and it looked like it might catch on fire. He dragged me from the car and put me down in the grass as I continued to panic. "NO, I HIT SOMEBODY! WHO DID I HIT?!"

1

## TRAGEDY TO TRUTH

The grass was cold. The dew had set in and the fog was lowering. I kept trying to sit up as I watched Blake run to the front of my car. What just happened? What had I done? Blake came back from the front of my car, ran past me, and jumped a 4-foot fence separating my parents' cul-de-sac and the road I was lying next to.

Other people began jumping the fence, and chaos erupted in the strange silence as I fought to stay conscious. I heard screaming, crying, and someone was yelling, "He's not breathing!"

Firemen began to arrive at the scene. The one who was administering first aid to me started asking me a lot of questions, but I was knocked on the head pretty hard and too confused to answer most of them. I could tell the fireman was greatly disturbed by the situation, and he was pretty rough with me. "Is my friend OK?" I asked. He snapped back at me, "I'm not worrying about him right now. I'm worrying about you."

I remember my dad, a lawyer, leaning into my ear and whispering, "Don't say anything!" My dad was a helicopter pilot and a veteran who had served in Vietnam. Later, he told me that what he saw at that scene was worse than anything he had seen during his time in the war.

I lay in the grass, covered in glass and blood. I was unable to move much on my own. I was terrified and I didn't know what was going to happen. As they put me in the ambulance, I heard my sister let out an awful, bloodcurdling scream as the ambulance doors closed. She had arrived on the scene, saw my car, and thought I was dead.

When we got to the hospital, they immediately began brushing the glass off, running tests, asking questions, and trying to figure out if I had any major internal injuries. My father was there with me the entire time telling anyone who asked me a non-medical question that I was not going to say anything.

2

## THE CRASH

I kept asking the same two questions to my dad, nurses, and practically anyone else. "Who did I hit? Is he OK?" I had narrowed it down to either James or John, and I wanted to know if he was okay, but no one would tell me anything. I was desperate and frustrated.

Over the next few hours, doctors and nurses tended to me. The sterile smell of the hospital mixed with the stench of drying blood in my nostrils. I faded in and out of consciousness, but for the most part they kept me awake.

At one point, they took me in for a CT scan to make sure I didn't have any serious internal injuries. A police officer came along to "help" them. Later, I realized that since I was going to be charged as a criminal, they wanted to keep an eye on me. When I got into the room and they moved me from the gurney to the table for the scan, a matchbox fell out of my pocket. The police officer asked me if there was any pot in it. Fortunately, there wasn't, and I told him he could look if he wanted. He asked me how much I had to drink.

I responded, "I want my lawyer."

He immediately back-peddled and said that would not be necessary; that he was just wondering.

Not long after I returned to the emergency room from my CT scan, a tall State Trooper walked into my hospital room. The darkness of his uniform and the formality of his tone left little doubt as to why he was there. He said, "Son, I need to have your blood tested. There has been a fatality." Finally, someone answered my question. My friend, John, was dead.

When the shocking news fully registered, and I realized what I had done, I began to sob. I thought about all of the times John and I had spent at the coffee shop with our friends. Just a few weeks ago, he had talked me through my break-up with my girlfriend.

A million questions rushed through my mind in a swirl of chaos and disorder. What had I done? What would his parents do? How would they go on? Would I go to prison? Would my parents go to prison?

I never meant for this to happen. The gravity of the news pressed hard against my chest. I could not believe this was happening. John was my friend, and I had killed him.

## DISCUSSION QUESTIONS – THE CRASH

1. What traumatic events have you faced in life that caused you and others pain?

2. When tragedy strikes, are you more prone to anxiety or faith? How has this played out in your life?

3. Unimaginable pain can be caused as a result of sin. How does Casey's story make you feel about the sinful attitudes you harbor?

4. How willing are you to allow the Lord to apply His truth to your tragedy?

## CHAPTER 2

# BEGINNINGS

Every story starts somewhere, but the tragic accident that took my friend's life is not where my story begins. I didn't just wake up one day, a post-puberty, wayward teenager with a drinking problem who decided to go out for a joyride. No, what happened that night had been building for a very long time.

## A BOY AND HIS DAD

I know it sounds cliché to say that my story begins with my relationship with my dad. I mean, come on; haven't there been enough books written about the importance of the bond between a boy and his dad?

I'll answer my own question. Yes, there have been.

And while this isn't a book about the importance of that bond, my relationship with my dad **is important** to my story, and provides a good bit of background to it, so I'll start there.

Let me begin by taking a moment to honor both of my parents. I am a grown man, a dad myself, and I am sure that somewhere down the road, if I haven't already done it, I am going to make mistakes that will affect my children's perception of God, of themselves and of the world they live in. Parents aren't perfect, mine included, me included. This isn't intended to discredit or dishonor them in any way. It just sheds light on the lifetime of events and emotions that led me to that fateful night.

# BY THE BOOK

My dad was a no nonsense kind of guy, having been raised himself by a no nonsense kind of guy. Ex-military, turned lawyer, my dad was by-the-book, all about rules, regulations, and structure. We did things a certain way, his way, because his way was the only way. As I got older, his intensity level chilled out some, but in my early years, it was tangible. At least it seemed that way through my young eyes.

Though he was often distant, when we interacted he was direct and demanding. Despite all that, deep down in my soul, I wanted nothing more than to please him. I not only **wanted** his approval, I **desperately needed it.**

I'm not saying he was a flawed individual who withheld his love and encouragement from me. In fact, I think he tried very hard to be encouraging. It's just that so very often his encouragement came across as an admonishment.

If I made a 96 on a test, he'd jokingly say, "What? You couldn't make a 100?" I knew he was *trying* to be encouraging and I knew he was joking, but it still resonated the message that once again I had not been good enough or met his expectations.

One time when I played baseball, he called me over and told me that if I would just hit it out of the park we'd win the game. The only problem was, I had never hit it over the fence, not once, not even close. So instead of being empowered, I was filled with anxiety, knowing I would not meet his expectations, and he'd be disappointed.

## BEGINNINGS

Over and over, in big ways and small ways, I felt like I would never measure up to his expectations.

My dad wanted me to be a tough kid, but I was emotional and at times, dramatic. He wanted me to be a star athlete, but I was pretty average at most sports I tried. He wanted me to be a great student, but I struggled academically most of my life. In every way that it mattered to him, I always felt like I was a disappointment to my dad.

I know my mom sensed the discord in our relationship and did what any good mom would do. She overcompensated. So while my dad was demanding, my mom was permissive. If my dad punished me for something, my mom was right there to let me off the hook. She made excuses for my dad's behavior, and she made excuses for mine.

And such was the cycle of our family dynamics.

## CHAPTER 3

# EARLY YEARS

I looked up from the place where I stood next to my first grade teacher's desk, wiping my sleeve across my mouth and desperately hoping that somehow all of my classmates had mysteriously disappeared. As I cautiously opened my eyes, I realized that my worst nightmare had in fact, come true. I had thrown up in my teacher's trashcan in front of my entire class.

That morning, I found a bottle of aftershave that I had received in my Christmas stocking and thrown on a little for a boost of extra confidence, you know, "Home Alone" style. But when I entered my classroom, I soon realized that my extra boost of confidence had drawn the attention of everyone in my class, but not in the way I had hoped. The boost of confidence quickly became a boost of terror. I stunk.

The teacher, in her search for the source of the terrible odor, mistakenly blamed a girl sitting in front of me, a fact that sent me running for the bathroom, both in distress and in relief. Distressed over the fact that an innocent girl had been blamed and relieved that I had not been found out and forever known as the smelly kid.

## TRAGEDY TO TRUTH

But try as I might, that stupid aftershave was not coming off, no matter how hard I scrubbed. Finally, red-skinned and nauseous, I returned to class, only to feel that all-too-familiar wave of anxiety come over me, and up it came.

Right there in front of everyone.

Man, I was a bright little kid, insanely shy, always obsessively worried or anxious, often to the point of making myself feel like I was going to be sick. My worst nightmare was that I would throw up in class and my classmates would ridicule me for my entire elementary career (a worry so real that it became a self-fulfilling prophecy). I was seriously one worried, messed up kid.

I don't mean worried as in "worried I wouldn't get that new bike I was hoping for, or worried I wouldn't get to watch my favorite cartoon." No I mean a deep-seated sense of doom that threatened to overtake my mind on a regular basis.

And I didn't just worry about things as though they "might" occur;I was haunted by these things as though they were imminent.

I constantly worried that my parents would get divorced or die and I'd end up living with my grandparents.

I worried that someone would break into our house in the middle of the night. (And remember, I didn't just worry like a little kid afraid of the dark. I worried as if I had direct knowledge that someone would be sneaking through our back door in the middle of the night.)

So I rarely slept.

Like most little kids, I had a very active imagination; but unlike most children, my active imagination was a torture chamber that often held me hostage in my own little world of "what ifs."

I hated feeling out of control and anxious and worried, but as a child, those emotions were a part of my daily life.

EARLY YEARS

Eventually the constant barrage of anxiety wore me down and led to depression. By third grade (yes, third grade) my depression was so severe that my parents took me to see a psychologist.

## A CHANGE FOR THE BETTER

Eventually, my parents concluded that it would be best to pull me out of the larger public school setting I was in, and place me in a smaller, private Christian school for the remainder of my elementary years. In that small group of nine kids, I really came out of my shell and learned to mask my overwhelming anxiety with a great sense of humor.

It was also there that I learned about God. I learned that Jesus loved me, but I didn't really understand why. It was hard to grasp why a guy thousands of years before would give a rip about me, my anxiety, my worries, or anything having to do with me at all. Other than praying when I needed something, I didn't really get the whole "God" thing.

At best, I believed that God was distant and demanding, much like my earthly father. So, not only was I trying to attain the approval of my dad, I was also now fearfully trying to live in view of a distant, yet demanding God, one who would punish me if I was bad, and leave me alone if I was doing well. God wasn't part of my daily life; a fact that would have weighty consequences down the road.

## QUESTIONS

1. Have you ever struggled with anxiety or depression as a young person? How did this affect your life?

2. Looking back on your childhood, what characteristics or personality traits do you see as a common thread in your life? Are they helpful or destructive?

11

## TRAGEDY TO TRUTH

3. What role, if any, do you think your relationship with your parents played in any of this? Have you come to terms with these feelings? If so, how? And if not, why not?

4. What was your first experience with church like? Did you find it to be helpful, confusing, boring, comforting? Why?

CHAPTER 4

# PEOPLE PLEASERS OF THE WORLD, PLEASE STAND UP

Like every middle school kid, I was embarrassed and humiliated often. Girls dumped me; I was beat up in the locker room; I was awkward and thought about sex all the time. I also had a strong need to be respected and accepted by all. Though what I experienced in middle school was not unusual, it impacted my life profoundly. I was determined to gain respect and avoid humiliation at all costs . . . a pattern that would follow me throughout my childhood and adolescence.

Early on, I figured out what people wanted or needed from me, and I gave it to them. The more I learned how to manipulate people by pretending to be what they wanted, the more confidence I gained outwardly. The more confidence I gained, the more people were attracted to me. And the more people were attracted to me, the more I wanted to please them. It was a vicious cycle to say the least.

By all outward appearances, I had it together.

But that was on the outside. On the inside, I was the same anxious kid I had always been. And the more I worked at being whom others expected me to be, the more of myself I lost, and the more I slipped into the darkness of fear and depression.

# MIDDLE SCHOOL

I stood terrified with my sister under the area where the busses dropped off kids. There was a throng of kids, many much larger than me. And while I was pretty big for a 6th grader, the other middle school kids seemed huge by comparison. Some of them had beards, and I think one even pulled into the parking lot driving his own car to school. I was no longer in my sheltered, private school environment, that's for sure. I was in a jungle full of hormonal pre-teens. Hello middle school and good-bye to Casey.

For the first several weeks of middle school, I was lonely. Most of the kids had attended elementary school together and seemed to be a close-knit and closed-off group of friends. I wanted so desperately to be liked and approved by my peers, that I spent the next several years of my life gaining their approval, a fact that proved to be my undoing in more ways than one.

I remember early on in my new middle school experience, I told a lie about beating up a bully-of-a-kid named Baylor. Baylor was a small kid and though I was way bigger than him, it did not keep him from picking on me all of the time when we were younger.

My problem was that I was like Ralphy in 'A Christmas Story' when he got in a fight with the redheaded kid. Just like Ralphy, when I got mad, I cried. It was like an instinct. I wasn't scared or anything, I just cried.

Well one day, a year or two before Middle School, Baylor was messing with me at baseball practice and I finally got tired of it. He tried to hit my hat off of my head, but he lightly hit my nose in the process. Because I had always been taught not to

## PEOPLE PLEASERS OF THE WORLD, PLEASE STAND UP

throw the first punch, but could hit back if I was hit first, I took that as a "hit" (call it a loophole). So red-faced, angry and crying, I hauled off and punched him hard in the arm. His dad turned around and because he knew Baylor could be a bully, made him run a lap and didn't make me do anything. I felt justified.

When I retold it to some of the kids at my new school, I embellished the story a little, leaving out the parts about me crying of course. What better way to fit in than to be seen as a tough guy who can take down bullies?

Unfortunately, even though Baylor had moved away the summer before, some of the kids knew him well and called him over the weekend to verify my story. The following Monday in class I was exposed as a liar and pronounced "unlikeable" by one of the popular girls in our class. I was devastated, having gotten what I deserved for lying; but even more determined to please this new group of people in my life.

## THE A TEAM

Sixth graders weren't allowed to play organized sports for the school, but they did have intramural sports. I was on a team that made it to the finals in a sport that was like Ultimate Frisbee, but with a ball. I don't remember what it was called, but we were in the finals.

My team was great, and I started being "that guy" who pumped the crowd up. I really got them going. They were going crazy for the 6A team, and my ability to connect with people made my popularity soar. The more I stood out from the crowd and the more confident I seemed, the more people liked me.

Equally important to me was the attention I was getting from my dad for being popular. He even took me to get a "cool kid" makeover, complete with a haircut and a pair of jeans so trendy it would have made Zack Morris stand up and take notice.

15

## TRAGEDY TO TRUTH

And of course, with my new look and my newly found popularity, I was also a hit with the ladies (well, as much of a hit as any 6th grader can be). I even experienced my first opened-mouth kiss in a scandalous game of truth or dare with a girl named Heather. (I wonder how many people have had their first kiss courtesy of a game of truth or dare?)

By 7th grade I had progressed from star baseball player to star football player, where I excelled at guarding the quarterback (who just happened to be my good friend, Marvin).

> *"Funny aside: one of my more memorable ADD moments happened during our first scrimmage football game. I told the coach that the defense was slow getting off of the line, so I suggested we go on "Set" instead of "Hike". He said it was a good idea, so that was the plan. Marvin got up on me and said, "Down, Set..." and the offensive line jumped into the defense. It would have been a brilliant play, because the defense wasn't expecting it. However, I forgot to snap the ball on "Set", so we got an offside penalty, I got laughed at by my coach and a helmet slap. I was so embarrassed and felt like a complete idiot."*

By 8th grade, my friends and I were the kings on campus. We were 8th graders, popular and looked up to by all, even the teachers and the school staff. And though not all of the kids in the group were "that cool", collectively we were the people that the crowd wanted to be with. We were the people that the head bangers made fun of. We were the popular people (and I think even the head bangers secretly liked us).

## PEOPLE PLEASERS OF THE WORLD, PLEASE STAND UP

My transition from awkward, shy, insecure little kid had taken place in my early school years and by the end of middle school, I had morphed into the man everyone wanted me to be. I was a ladies' man, a mama's boy, and the teacher's pet.

I was my own professional image manager; not concerned about who I wanted to be, but always focused on what others wanted from me. I had already learned, far too early in life, that few people like you for who you are and are more concerned with what benefit they can get from you.

# LIVING A LIE

Like I said, on the outside, I had it all together. But the inside told a completely different story. Despite my growing popularity, I was miserable on the inside, living a lie every single day of my life.

The truth is depression was my reality. By 13 years of age, I was in a very dark place and stuck in an identity crisis. My depression was fueled by years and years of anxiety and fear and feelings that were slowly turning into anger, especially as they mixed with the flood of hormones I was experiencing. I was constantly angry, and increasingly more focused on fooling around with girls.

By the end of 8th grade, I was watching my dad's porn videos, I was sexually active (but mostly just heavy petting at this point), and I was overcome by lust and the guilt that goes along with it.

My life was defined by frustration and anger. And even though I had everything a kid could want, I often felt alone and misunderstood.

The outcome of living a lie, of trying to please others, of being something you're not every single day of your life takes a toll. And I was certainly paying the price.

# A CHRISTIAN BY THE BOOK

My life as a Christian was in the same miserable shape as the rest of my life. In the spring of 1990, I went to a class at a United Methodist church called Confirmation. It was supposed to be a sixteen-week course where we learned about the Christian faith, and if we agreed to all they taught, we would be confirmed. As an 11 year-old that had been to church on and off for several years, I assumed that since my parents and my sister were Christians, then I must be one too. After all, I went to church, I prayed, and I owned a Bible.

Of the sixteen classes, I went to about four of them. (That's twenty-five percent attendance. Typically, if you only attend twenty-five percent of any class you would fail, but I passed!) One Sunday morning, my mom told me that I was going to be baptized at church, so I went. All the other kids had shawls they had made on a retreat that I did not go on. So, I got a blank one and drew a cross on it with a pencil to look more religious. It was interesting, to say the least.

We went up on stage and the leaders held up signs with answers we were to have to the questions, "I will, I will, I do, I will." After that, they went around and sprinkled our heads with water and that was it. By the book, I was officially a Christian. And since I went to church a few times each year and did religious stuff, I considered myself a pretty good one.

PEOPLE PLEASERS OF THE WORLD, PLEASE STAND UP

## DISCUSSION QUESTIONS

1. What people or experiences influenced you the most during your pre-teen and early teenage years? Did these influences cause you joy or pain, as you got older?

2. Who taught you about how to interact with the opposite sex? Was their influence biblical and constructive, or did it lead to heartache and sin?

3. Are you a "chameleon" who shifts your personality to appease others, or are you a more confident, independent person? How has this played a role in your spiritual life?

4. Do you ever find yourself obsessing over what people think of you? What gospel truths would bring freedom to you if you were able to fully believe them?

CHAPTER 5

# FITTING IN

I don't know very many people who would want to relive their high school years. It's not that the years are all bad; in fact, in many ways it's easy to look back and find truly great memories. It's just that as adults, when we look back on our high school years, what we tend to remember most is trying to find ourselves and figuring out how we fit into the world around us.

Fitting in, and the need to be a part of a community, isn't something we outgrow. Even as adults, we still have a strong desire to want to belong. It's a desire that's hard-wired into us by our Creator. But in high school, the desire to fit in easily can and often does become the MOST important thing.

Each year of high school was an introduction of sorts to some new experience, some new attempt at fitting in, until eventually all of my attempts failed, setting up the sequence of events that resulted in tragedy.

## FRESHMAN YEAR

My family had moved to the suburbs, a fact that meant we had to change schools, moving us away from the friends we had

## TRAGEDY TO TRUTH

gone to school with the previous years. Our mom agreed to keep working at her job in our old school district (even though the job was incredibly hard on her) just so my sister and I could attend the high school we wanted to attend.

But man, was high school different than middle school. By the end of middle school, I was the 'man'; very popular, Vice President of the Student Council, with a ton of friends. Here, in this monstrosity of a high school though, I was extremely overwhelmed. I was a nobody and that reality weighed on me in a very real way.

On the first day of school, in science class, I sat next to a guy wearing red who informed me he was in a gang. A gang. I lived in the burbs, where the very mention of the word "gang" terrified people and here I was with first-hand access to a gangster. This kid was 14 years old and had been in the gang over a year. He told me of the violence he had endured, along with the loyalty in community that he experienced in his gang. He was a part of something that really mattered, at least to him. And while "belonging" sounded great, I knew it was not the life I wanted.

Still, it was a struggle finding my way there. I didn't know any of the kids from other schools, so I hung out with my close friends from middle school the first few days. But after our first week, I was completely worn out and not looking forward to the next four years.

My sister, on the other hand, had reconnected with her old friends and was doing her thing. One night, she went to a pool party put on by the school's dance team, a place you'd think would be a safe, well-chaperoned event. But while she was there, she was surrounded by a group of football players and assaulted. I still remember her coming home that night after it happened. And I still remember the feelings of hatred that welled up inside of me towards the young men who had assaulted her.

At this point my anxiety and depression were still there, but I had been seeing a psychologist for a while and was getting better at dealing with it . . . until now. The anger had been brewing for several years, an undercurrent, existing just below the surface, and my sister's assault caused it to reach a boiling point. The young men who had assaulted my sister didn't look like me, so it was easy to learn to hate them. And once I gave into my anger and hatred toward them, it seemed to make it easy to feel anger and hatred towards people of races different than mine.

## MAKING A CHANGE

We had a high school within walking distance from our house, so my parents withdrew us from the school we were attending and moved us to the one closer to our home. Our new school had not yet started, so it was an easy change, especially considering the things that had happened at our old school.

The high school I attended initially was very diverse. There were people from all backgrounds and nationalities. However, the high school we transferred to was much different. I went from a melting pot to a snowstorm. It was almost entirely white people.

As I walked into the gymnasium for freshman orientation at this new school, I felt ahead of the game since I had already spent a week in a much larger, more dangerous high school. Still, I was very lonely. I knew a couple of baseball friends from last year, but by and large all of these kids went to the same middle school and knew each other. I was a 'new kid' and an outsider.

## FAMILIAR THINGS

When I registered for classes, I asked to be put into the baseball PE class. Baseball was familiar to me, something I knew. And

## TRAGEDY TO TRUTH

when the things around you feel uncertain and unfamiliar, anything that feels remotely familiar is comforting. So on the first day of class, I arrived to the athletic field house on the last period and was informed that they did not allow freshman to be a part of the baseball class. Awesome. So much for comfort and familiarity.

They went on to tell me if I wanted to play baseball, it would be good for me to play football to get to know some of the coaches.

Football.

Great.

I didn't like football, wasn't great at it and was not really excited to play. I had asthma, and had quit the football team the year before. I was scared that I would not perform well, and would be embarrassed.

However, I wanted to play baseball, so I reluctantly agreed to be on the football team. I practiced for four days, but on the day of the first game I went home "sick" from school and skipped the game, forcing my parents to pull me from the football team. Unfortunately, this meant I had to be moved to what was known as "the reject" PE class.

I think in some ways, though, I felt like maybe I belonged there.

Despite those early weeks of trying to find some familiarity in my new surroundings, I did eventually make friends.

Just before Christmas break, several of us had gone to dinner and were driving back in the rain. As we came up over a large overpass heading into town, we realized the traffic was stopped, but the girl driving was not able to stop in time. She slammed on the brakes, and we slammed into the back of another car. Immediately she started panicking, so I climbed out of the car from the backseat and helped her see what kind of damage had been done.

It was cold outside and she was wearing a thin shirt. I was wearing a t-shirt and a large jacket, so I gave her my jacket to wear, and stood in the cold rain wearing just a t-shirt. At the time, my neck felt a little stiff, but I didn't really think anything of it. But once I got home and took off my wet shirt, it was like something froze in my upper back. We had a family friend who was a doctor, and he saw me that night because I was in severe pain. Apparently I had whiplash in my neck and back, and had also bruised my spleen. I was laid up in bed for a few weeks and missed a lot of school, including finals.

When I returned after Christmas Break, I had a lot of make-up work to do and had to spend several Saturdays making up my absences in Saturday School. As much as I hated school, I now had to spend four additional hours sitting in a quiet room either reading, writing, or doing homework. It was absolute torture for any kid, but especially for a kid with learning disabilities, and I had to spend six consecutive Saturday's doing this in order to make up my time.

# A SLIPPERY SLOPE

One of the ways I dealt with my learning disabilities was to cheat on homework and exams. I was taking Spanish and having a hard time memorizing all of the vocabulary words. Since failing was not an option in my home, and I would do pretty much anything to avoid my dad's disappointment, I learned to make double-sided cheat sheets the size of the palm of my hand. One day, I was taking a quiz and got busted cheating.

The teacher called me out into the hall, and when she turned her back, I balled up the paper and swallowed it. There was no chewing, no stashing it in my cheek, I just straight-up swallowed it. By the time we got into the hall, she asked to see my hands, which were of course, clean. She searched my mouth

# TRAGEDY TO TRUTH

and then asked me what I was looking at. I told her, "Nothing." (The scene in my head is much funnier now than it was then. Trust me.)

She sent me back to my seat, shaken up, but emboldened to cheat. Another class I cheated my way through was Physical Science. I had a friend give me all of his returned tests that I missed because of the accident. They were all multiple choice, so I wrote out the answers to the exams on small pieces of paper. I made 100's on almost all of them, but I purposefully missed a few on occasion, so as not to raise suspicion.

At first, I felt guilty about all the cheating, but as it became a regular habit, I justified it as a necessary evil. I didn't want people to know how dumb I felt, and I didn't want my parents being disappointed in me. Looking back, it seems like the cheating took a lot more time and effort than actually taking the time to learn the content of the subject.

Funny thing about making and then justifying bad decisions;it's a slippery slope that makes it much easier to continue making and then justifying other bad decisions.

Early that spring I was invited to join a group of friends for a sleep over. These guys were on the football team now, but I knew them from the year before in baseball. The house we stayed at had a game room upstairs with old-school arcade games, and they were free! We were hanging out, playing video games, and doing what most typical high school kids do. Eventually my friend asked if I wanted a beer. I had already been sneaking swigs off his mom's wine in their upstairs wet bar fridge, so I said, "Sure."

I wasn't sure where he was going to get the beer since it was close to midnight, and I knew that none of us had fake ID's. Turns out, his dad had a large fridge in the garage that he kept stocked with beer. Every now and then, my friend stole a few beers until eventually he had his own stash in the garage. He

# FITTING IN

brought each of us a couple of hot beers. I remember drinking it and how it made me feel, and I liked it.

I knew that night that alcohol was going to play a bigger part in my plan to be who I thought everyone wanted me to be.

Like I said, it's a slippery slope.

A few weeks later we went back to the same friend's house, but this time I took along my own contribution of alcohol (at my friend's request). My sister and I had found a box full of liquor in our garage that my dad had been given as gifts over the years. I snagged a bottle of Scotch and took it with me. I remember trying the Scotch and it how awful it tasted, but the other guys started showing off by chugging it. I told them to be careful, but they ignored me and chugged large amounts of alcohol until the bottle was empty.

In no time at all, they were acting drunk. They were football players, dancing around the room, mooning each other, and giggling like a bunch of little girls. After a few more minutes, one of my friends, who had chugged the most scotch, turned pale and without any warning vomited all over our friend's bedroom wall. It was disgusting, and we were scared that my friend's parents were about to find out.

Apparently my friend's mom heard the thud of someone falling to the ground and us reacting to his massive amount of vomit, so she came upstairs. We were busted. I begged my friends not to rat me out for bringing the alcohol, and I told them that if my parents found out that I would be dead, or at least sent to military school. I'm not sure if that really would have happened, but I had enough fear and passion to convince them. Apparently, they made up a story, or at least convinced their parents not to tell my parents.

Fearing my parents might find out what had happened at the party, I gave them my own version of the story. I told my parents there had been alcohol at the party, but I didn't drink any, which was a lie, but they believed me. I felt so guilty and was terrified they would find out the truth. I felt sick for weeks and was scared about what would happen if they ever found out. It put a huge strain on my friendship with this group of guys. I never really knew why, but I assume they lost respect for me for my unwillingness to take responsibility for bringing the liquor in the first place. Looking back, I don't blame them. I behaved like a coward.

# FINDING MY WAY

In the spring, I tried out for the baseball team but ended up getting cut.

Fortunately, my Algebra teacher was also the swim coach and had taken a liking to me. When she asked me if I wanted to be on the swim team, I told her that I was good at freestyle and would love to be on the team, though I had never spent a day in my life on a swim team. But hey, I really liked to swim, and I hated my current PE class, so her invitation seemed like a way out of the reject class. The team only had a few weeks left at the pool, so we got my schedule changed, and I joined the swim team. I only went to a few practices and my "asthma" acted up. Looking back I think I was just really out of shape and didn't know how to swim correctly. My teacher mercifully proposed that I could be a manager for the swim team.

Things went south with the swim coach though when my swim team friends and I were playing touch football one day. One of the older swimmers intentionally pushed me and I got up and pushed him back, ready to throw down. She didn't like that aggression, apparently, so I was no longer welcome in that class, and back I went to reject PE.

In many ways this felt like rejection, and I began to feel like I really belonged with the rejects. Back in middle school I had

# FITTING IN

been popular and had a lot of friends, but at the new school, I felt so out of place.

As it turned out, getting kicked off the swim team, and being cut from the baseball team opened an unexpected door for me.

Weeks earlier, I had performed a portion from a play in my theatre class and did really well. My theatre teacher asked me if I wanted to be involved with the One Act play competition. At the time, I was busy trying out for the baseball team, so I couldn't do it. After I was cut, I went to her and asked if they needed any help. She was very kind and allowed me to be an understudy. It was the first time I was involved with something that seemed to fit really well.

An understudy is someone who shadows the actors, learns their lines, and fills in when the actors are absent. When I wasn't understudying, I was a crew member, which meant I had to help move set pieces around, pick up costumes, and do other grunt work. For the first time since middle school, I felt like I belonged with a group, even if we were a little weird.

The kids in theatre were kind, accepting, and creative. Some were conforming to non-conformity, some were serious about acting, and others were looking for a place to belong. I got nervous reading scripts out loud because of my undiagnosed learning disabilities, but I still had a lot of fun and soon excelled in theatre.

## DISCUSSION QUESTIONS

1. Has anyone close to you ever been abused or assaulted? How did it make you feel...angry, scared, depressed? How did you respond to these emotions?

2. What was your first introduction to alcohol or drugs like? Did you learn about them from your parents,

your friends, or media? How did your first experiences influence you later?

3. If you close your eyes and imagine what a young person who loves Jesus would be like, what comes to mind? Do you feel like Jesus can create this kind of young person?

# SOPHOMORE YEAR

I spent a lot of time with my friends the summer after my freshman year. We went fishing almost every day in one of my friend's neighborhoods. Towards the end of the summer, I started dating a girl nicknamed "D". She was a sweet girl who smoked cigarettes and fell "in love" easily, but she had dated some rough guys in the past.

We were together for just a couple of months. She was needy and didn't really care about school, even less than me. I knew things were getting weird when I was diagnosed with mono and told her that we couldn't kiss anymore. She said she wanted to kiss me so that she could be sick with me. What in the world?! That was too weird, so I broke up with her not long after that.

Behind a grocery store one day that summer, I had my first cigarette. This wasn't the brightest move because of my asthma, but I wanted to see what the big deal was. I don't even think I finished the cigarette, because I thought I wouldn't be a "smoker" as long as I didn't finish the whole cigarette.

That fall, I got drunk for the first time at my friend Kyle's house. His parents went out of town and left him by himself, so he frequently had parties. One night, I drank a 40 oz. bottle of Mickey's Malt Liquor and got pretty drunk. There was a pretty girl there who I knew casually, and I spent the rest of the night trying to get her to make out with me. I acted drunker than I

FITTING IN

was so that she would 'take care of me'. Once I realized that she wasn't going to put out, I moved on to another girl.

The other girl was "D", the girl I had broken up with a few months before. When I saw her at the party, I went up to her and kissed her. That was a risky move, but she reciprocated. It didn't take long for her to get on my nerves, so I spent the rest of the night trying to avoid her. She didn't take too kindly to that, for obvious reasons.

Smoking, drinking, and caffeine-induced insomnia did nothing to help my depression or anxiety, not to mention being over six weeks behind in school because of Mono. I had a tutor that came to my house a few times a week, but it was hard for me to learn from her. She had complications with hearing and, as a result, her speech was slurred. She was a sweet lady though and, if I acted like I understood what she was saying, she left sooner. Let's just say I was good at acting.

# TROUBLE AT HOME

My older sister was a senior in high school by this time, and she butted heads with my parents way more than I did. She required so much of their attention that I slid by essentially ignored, a fact I really didn't mind. I felt like I could take care of myself, especially when I started to realize that my parents had serious problems of their own. My dad had overcommitted us financially by buying our house a few years back and it was catching up with him. We had to give our cars back to the banks, and weren't able to buy new clothes, which was a big deal in high school. Wearing old clothes was like wearing a scarlet letter…"P" for poor."

This new level of "poverty" was unlike anything I had known until this point in my life. I lived in an area surrounded by wealth, and we were barely able to make our mortgage

TRAGEDY TO TRUTH

payments. It was at this point in my life that I began to believe that if I were truly going to be taken care of, I would have to do it on my own. I thought I couldn't rely on anyone but myself.

I had just returned from a school trip to a theatre conference where I tried LSD for the first and last time. Everyone told me that it was going to be awesome, but I didn't like it. All it did was make me stay up all night and caused me to be paranoid. I regretted doing it immediately, but there wasn't anything I could do to reverse it. My parents never knew about my LSD experience, but my foolish decisions were mounting up and I was trying more and more risky behaviors in order to try to fit in with the people around me.

# UNCOMMITTED

During the fall musical auditions, I sat behind a girl I knew from some of my classes named Sarah. She had a good friend named Kristie who had a big smile and was kind enough to laugh at my jokes. Kristie was everything opposite of my life. She was brilliant, excelled at everything she did, had a steady family life, and her family had money. I, on the other hand, was barely getting by in school, would rather sit at the coffee shop talking than studying, my family-life was unsteady, and, while we looked like we were doing well financially, we were on the brink of bankruptcy.

Kristie and I began talking on the phone a lot and eventually became a couple. She had invited me over to watch Beverly Hills 90210 and Melrose Place for her birthday. That's when I could really tell she liked me. I genuinely liked her too. We could have been great friends, but when romance entered in it elevated my insecurities and led me to be confrontational and insecure. She was driven by her desire to become a doctor, and I had nothing to be as passionate about.

## FITTING IN

My lack of passion and commitment for anything constructive really bothered and embarrassed me, but I just couldn't muster the conviction to care deeply about anything other than being liked and having fun.

Even my attempts at being a committed Christian were lukewarm, if that. I believed that I was a Christian because I had been to church and had been through some religious rituals, but at this point in my life, I really began to doubt the existence of God. My friend, Mike, read a book about how aliens had placed us on this planet, and he was convinced it was true. His arguments were convincing to me since I had no strong religious foundation. Seriously, I wish I were kidding. But I actually gave some serious consideration to believing his argument. Eventually, I tried to convince myself that religion was about being a good person, feeling at peace, and being nice to other people, but that just left me feeling empty and more confused.

# GIVING UP

By the second semester of my sophomore year, my depression returned with a vengeance. I was behind on the work I missed the first semester when I was sick, I had started partying more, and I wanted to drop out of high school. I actually skipped a few days with my friend, Chris. Chris had dropped out earlier that year and seemed to be doing okay.

My parents acknowledged that I was having a hard time, but they weren't sure how to help me. So they took me back to the psychologist I had seen over the years, and she referred me to a male psychologist in her office. He suggested finding an alternative private school for me to go to so that I could catch up on my work. Great. I'd be going to a school for rejects. I wasn't sure what was worse, dropping out and getting an alternative diploma or going to the reject school.

## TRAGEDY TO TRUTH

My parents decided to try the school for rejects. It was called River Oaks Academy, which sounded fancy since River Oaks is a wealthy area in Houston. However, the school was not in River Oaks. It was in the hood. To be honest, this school was a joke. It was more about doing your time than actually learning anything.

I met a guy there named Truman, who was absolutely hilarious. I thought if I could have had an older brother, I would've wanted this guy. He was so fun to hang out with, and he got in all kinds of trouble. We started hanging out sometimes after school and partied together on occasion.

In spite of all of our financial troubles, I had saved up enough money to buy a new Jeep Cherokee. Well, I saved enough to make a down payment on one. I poured the rest of my money into putting in a nice stereo system with large subwoofers, new rims and tires, and purple neon lights underneath it. I couldn't drive it for several months because I didn't have my license, so Truman and I just sat in it and turned the stereo up.

Truman helped me not take things so seriously, but he also instilled in me a greater disrespect for those in authority.

As the year went on, my anger continued to grow, and I began to direct it towards my father. I had been convinced for a few years that he didn't love me; that he tolerated me but only because I was his son. It's not that I can point out any one thing that made me feel this way, but I felt like he was annoyed with me a lot.

At the peak of my depression, I began to have suicidal thoughts. One night when I was very upset-I don't remember what set me off- I went downstairs and got my dad's shotgun out of the hall closet and told him, "If you want me to be dead, then I'll do it for you!"

I was out of control, so the psychologist sent me to a psychiatrist who put me on medication. This medicine made me

FITTING IN

chill out…a lot. It curbed my suicidal thoughts and outbursts, but I was less motivated than ever before to do anything. In spite of all of this craziness, Kristie stuck around and stayed with me.

## DISCUSSION QUESTIONS

1.  Do you ever feel your pride is injured by not having as much money or nice things as others around you? What do you think this reveals about your heart?

2.  Have disappointments or failures caused by other people led you to adopt a self-sufficient attitude? How does this kind of attitude affect your relationship with God?

3.  At any point in your spiritual life, have you had moments when you thought you were a Christian but started to wonder if you really knew what that meant? How did you respond to that doubt?

4.  Have you ever had suicidal thoughts or desires? If so, how does it make you feel to know that Jesus loves you enough that He gave up His life to save yours?

## JUNIOR YEAR

The summer after my sophomore year is a blur. I spent a lot of time with Kristie and the rest of the time in summer school making up all of the school I had missed. Somehow, I finished all of the work and made up all of the time, so I was able to be a junior the following year at the local high school instead of staying at River Oaks Academy. During this time, I played in a band called Blind Epitome. Dumb name, but we were playing some shows at nightclubs around Houston. I was the drummer,

## TRAGEDY TO TRUTH

but I was the manager as well. Playing in a band of teenage knuckleheads brought enough trouble of its own, but trying to manage the band was another anxiety-riddled pursuit.

I finally got my license and loved driving my Jeep, especially when neighbors complained because my speakers were causing their pictures to go crooked. However, one of my friends had a Camaro, so I decided I needed a Camaro. It took some convincing, but I was able to talk my dad into buying a 1995 Z-28 Camaro 6-speed with 275 horsepower stock. Trust me when I tell you, trading in a Cherokee for a Camaro is an incredible day in the life of a teenage boy.

# EMPTY

I had learned that even though they were struggling financially, my parents were willing to give me almost anything I asked for if I hounded them long enough. I had everything I wanted: my girlfriend, my friends, my car, my acting, and my band.

And yet, I was still miserable.

No matter what I added to my life, it never satisfied this gnawing hunger deep in my soul.

I tried religion and Agnosticism, but neither of those things seemed to fill in the gap in my heart. I tried pot a few times, but I felt very anxious every time I smoked it. Everyone else chilled out, but it only made me feel more paranoid. Pot seemed to be the solution for my friends, but for me it just made me continue to feel lost and lifeless.

Kristie and I were still together, but arguing a lot by this point. Maybe there were things she was doing that were bothering me, but I'm sure I was impossible to be with at this stage of my life. I got upset over the slightest thing, and argued until I couldn't remember what I was arguing about. I was miserable, and I wanted her to be miserable with me.

36

# FITTING IN

My parents let me have some parties at my house. They knew we were drinking alcohol, but thought that we would be safer at home rather than going out and drinking behind a building. It was their unspoken policy that they would not provide the alcohol, in order to maintain a level of deniability if anything happened. Kristie came to the parties, but since she didn't drink she drove home in time for curfew. I had tons of other people crashing at my house, but I went to bed alone to remain loyal to Kristie. It felt frustrating to have other people spending the night with their girlfriends while I went to bed by myself.

As much as I acted like all was well, I often laid in bed at night thinking to myself, "If this is all that there is, then I'd rather be dead." Despite the medication, suicidal thoughts were still haunting me on occasion, even with all of the "fun" I was having at the parties, driving my car, making out with my girlfriend, and acting in plays. No matter what I did, no matter what I thought or tried to believe, nothing was providing a lasting meaning or purpose. I was empty.

## DISCUSSION QUESTIONS

1   What are some things you are working to get (money, fun, relationships, social status, possessions, good grades)?

2.  After reading this chapter, how do you think differently about chasing after these things for fulfillment?

3.  How does it make you feel to be alone at any point? What do you think your response reveals about your heart?

4.  What sinful or destructive patterns would you point to in your life that you think could snowball into something you can no longer keep under control? What steps can you take now in order to avoid more heartache?

CHAPTER 6

# GALVESTON – THE CALM BEFORE THE STORM

The summer after my junior year, I took a job as a lifeguard. I wanted a job that would let me sit around a lot, (I had big goals) so I'm sure in my mind it seemed like lifeguarding would be an easy, glamorous job. Unfortunately my glamorous job lost its luster after just a few weeks, so I told my boss I needed to take a few weeks off. I had a friend whose family had a beach house in Galveston, and for some reason, we were able to talk our parents into letting us go there alone. It was June of 1995, and I was almost seventeen years old.

The trip to Galveston was a coming of age experience of sorts; it was my first time away from home for more than a day. For the first few days, the trip was incredible. We had a few friends over and started drinking beer and grilling burgers shortly after we arrived. The Houston Rockets were in The Finals and actually won the title while we were there. I didn't care much about basketball, but I did enjoy getting wrapped up in all of the hype.

We spent a lot of time on the beach talking about life, joking around, and being teenage boys on the verge of becoming men.

## SOMETHING BETTER

One night, a group of girls that my friend knew came over to hang out. I was not attracted to or interested in any of them, and still had a girlfriend at the time. However, I distinctly remember a conversation I had with one of the girls.

She was a few years younger than me and was getting pretty involved in drugs. While I had experimented a handful of times with marijuana and once with LSD, I was not a fan, and could easily see the devastation that drug addiction could cause.

Looking back, it's obvious I was a hypocrite. It was fine for me to binge drink, but by my way of thinking, this girl was out of her mind for doing drugs. For several hours, I sat and reasoned with her, trying to convince her to turn away from drugs and to embrace something better. I wasn't sure what was better, but I knew she was headed on a path for destruction.

I was good at looking out for myself, a skill I had honed to perfection, but rarely had I felt the need to look out for others. That night was different; I really wanted to help this girl. I didn't want her to throw her life away, and I didn't want her to end up dead. But while I was able to connect with her on an emotional level, I had no real message of hope to give her except, "Try hard and stay away from drugs."

Looking back, I wish I knew Jesus like I do now. I could have offered her something better. This girl was giving her life to the drugs, her idol, and if she continued to pursue it, it would leave her dead.

## FREEDOM

After wrapping up my drug-addiction counseling session, I had a few beers, and we went out to the beach with some plastic chairs. The beach was beautiful! The moon was huge and the

# GALVESTON – THE CALM BEFORE THE STORM

waves were small. I remember walking towards the slowly moving water and placing my chair in the sand. There was a feeling of peace that I had rarely felt before. The cool breeze on my face, the brightness of the moon, and the waves gently crashing against my legs was the most amazing feeling.

It was a moment of serenity that I never wanted to end. All of my anxiety, fear, and worry vanished for one moment, and in that moment, I had peace.

It was a sense of peace and quiet that I had not experienced before. I was someone who always needed to be around people, on the phone, or doing something. Learning to be still was not part of my upbringing and, for that brief moment, being still was what I needed. Although I was not yet a Christian, I considered myself spiritual and this was certainly a spiritual moment for me.

This peace, as enjoyable and memorable as it was, did not last. My plastic chair started sinking in the sand as the tide came in. As I pulled it out of the sand, the waves got a hold of it. It fell right against my left foot, tearing out a large chunk of flesh. I had been drinking, so it didn't hurt as badly as it should have. I could tell it was bleeding and my brilliant solution was to put it into the salt water of the ocean. Bad idea. The pain felt like a jellyfish sting, but I didn't want to leave the water.

I sat there for another half hour before my friends started heading back to the house. I reluctantly got up, picked up the chair, and limped back up the sandy path to the beach house. One disadvantage when traveling with other teenagers is that they don't prepare well. The beach house had most essentials, but there was no First Aid kit, so I had to do the best I could with some rags, paper towels, and water. My foot was throbbing, but I couldn't stop thinking about the peace I had just experienced on the beach. I felt free, if only for a moment, and it was something that I had never felt before.

## TRAGEDY TO TRUTH

Freedom was an idea, maybe even a made up god, which consumed most of the teenagers I knew. We wanted to be free from curfew, free from school, free from rules. The reality was, we wanted the benefits of adulthood, but not the responsibility. We wanted to be able to do whatever we wanted, but have no consequences. This seems like the typical plight of most teenagers I knew then, and the ones I know now. But the destructive decisions we make (teenagers and adults alike) often enslave us.

It's interesting how backwards we can get when we think we are experiencing freedom. Often, we are just freely going into slavery.

The feeling of freedom that I experienced that night is one that I have attempted to repeat many times since. Maybe that's where you are today; pursuing a sense of freedom and looking for increasingly better feelings and experiences?

# DISCUSSION QUESTIONS

1. Can you name any moments in your life when you distinctly felt like God was reaching out to you? How did you feel? How did you respond?

2. Do you feel like you have peace in your mind and heart? If so, where does your peace come from? If not, where are you looking for peace?

3. Do you find the commands of God to be freeing or enslaving? Why?

4. How can the pursuit of freedom from any authority at all actually enslave us?

## CHAPTER 7

# SELF-DESTRUCTING

We have all heard the old story called "The Boy Who Cried Wolf." The boy lies about seeing a wolf over and over again, and eventually no one believes him. One day there really is a wolf, and he cries out, but no one comes to his rescue, and he is eaten by the wolf.

For years, I had been that boy, always on the verge of self-destruction, until eventually no one believed it would really happen. But I did self-destruct, and in the midst of my own self-destruction, I killed someone. Someone who did believe me and came to my rescue.

## THE PARTY

**July 4th, 1995**

I could put on a great party. The first party I threw was in the 8th grade, and it was a huge success. I invited the kids from my middle school in my old neighborhood and some of my new friends from the new school. I knew how to have a good time, and more importantly, how to help other people have fun.

## TRAGEDY TO TRUTH

As I grew older, the parties I threw were much different than that first party. They were much more dangerous, much more out of control, with very few boundaries and very little supervision.

Just one month before the fateful night of July 4th, 1995, I had a blowout party that got completely out of hand. I was working as a lifeguard at the time and had friends who were either 21 or had fake IDs, allowing us all to chip in and buy a keg for the party. My parents had gone out for the afternoon, and I was able to sneak the keg upstairs without my parents seeing it.

Let's just say, the party got stupid very quickly.

Apparently, word got out that I was having a party, and we had over 100 people come to my house. Most of the people stayed upstairs with the keg, and the rest of the people were in the backyard. I had charged everyone $4, and by the end of the night I had almost $400 in cash. I almost got away with having a keg upstairs, but my idiot friends and I put the keg in a trashcan that happened to have holes in the bottom, so the melting ice in the trashcan formed a constant stream of water that soaked through the carpet and began leaking into my parents' bedroom around midnight. My dad was not happy, to say the least.

At the end of that night, I had made a tidy profit, but my house was trashed, and my parents made me stay up and clean the entire place. They also told me that I could not have any more parties.

But just one month later, I managed to convince my parents to let me have another party. I was a strong manipulator and wore my parents down, so on the 4th of July, in 1995, they gave in and let me have one more. My dad was inviting some friends over for the fourth and said I could have some friends over as well. I convinced him to buy a keg of beer for the party, arguing that it was far more economical than buying cases of beer. Then I called my friends and let them know we'd have a keg.

SELF-DESTRUCTING

# THE PARTY WAS ON

This time, I really meant to keep it low key. I only invited my closest friends from theatre, but, as it typically goes for high school parties, some friends told other friends, and there were over 20 people at my house before I knew it. Of course, it was not nearly as crazy as the previous party, but we were doing what we always did. We ate, drank beer, played hacky sack, and laughed together.

But this night and this party were not like other parties I'd had. Emotionally, I was in a really bad place. My girlfriend, Kristie, and I had broken up while I was on a theatre trip to Nebraska just a week before. She was going away to college and told me she didn't plan for us to continue being a couple after that. Since she was essentially breaking up with me, I beat her to the punch and broke it off with her that night.

I'd found a replacement girl while there on the trip to Nebraska, a dumb move on all accounts, as Mandi, the new girl, already had a boyfriend **and** she lived several states away. It had disaster written all over it.

All of this girl drama had taken place a week before this party, and I was in a really weird place. My girlfriend of a year-and-a-half was gone, my new girl was in Nebraska and still likely with that boyfriend of hers, and I was all alone.

I didn't like being alone.

I didn't like having no one to be with who gave me a feeling of worth.

Even though I constantly surrounded myself with people, I felt in my heart like I was on a deserted island. I thought having a party would cheer me up, but all it did was emphasize that while I had 'friends', that is, people my age who liked to do the same things that I did, I was still very alone.

Something about my feelings that night were just different. There's no real way for me to explain the depth of those feelings,

45

TRAGEDY TO TRUTH

the darkness of them. The loneliness I felt was different than I had ever felt before.

My life was changing. I was getting older, and I realized that those I thought I was close to, who I was around a lot, were not true friends. My relationships were all very shallow.

# UNRAVELING

On the night of the party, I was feeling lonely, depressed, and distant. I didn't want to be dramatic, but I didn't feel like being around people. At the same time, I also didn't feel like being alone. As the night went on, I tried to ask some of my closer friends, Mike and Esteban, if I could talk with them, but they said they had to leave to go talk about something. So, I did what I knew how to do best; I drank some beer and then looked around for a girl to fool around with.

There was a girl from a different high school there whom we were friends with. She and I flirted briefly a few years back at a theater conference, but it never went anywhere. I knew she still liked me, so I found her and started to flirt with her. We ended up in my bedroom with several other friends and started making out together. A guy kept asking me how her kisses tasted. To be honest they tasted a little like beer, cigarettes, and minty gum. Her lips were soft and I could tell she had feeling behind the kisses. I, however, didn't have any feeling, only guilt. I remember pretending to fall asleep or 'pass out' in order to create a defense for myself later on as to why I made out with her.

It's funny the things I remember about that fateful night.

After a while, someone came in my room and told me that Lauren was there. Lauren was my "first love," a girl from middle school that I still had feelings for. Again, it was all based on lust way more than love, but I left the girl I was making out with and went to find Lauren.

46

SELF-DESTRUCTING

I was feeling very insecure after breaking up with Kristie, and I wanted to be liked by someone as pretty as Lauren. Lauren was a brilliant girl. She was in honors classes, made straight A's, and had been a great volleyball player. Once I found her, we walked outside and talked on the driveway for a while. She told me about some guy she was talking to, but I didn't pay much attention to what she was saying. My only thoughts were on getting her to make out with me.

As we talked, she told me that she'd needed money and started dealing drugs. Not light drugs either, but heavy drugs. Something had changed in her, she was no longer the brilliant, sweet, and kind girl I grew up with. Now I saw her as some misguided, dope-dealing piece of white trash. I was pissed and very sad for her.

# COMING UNDONE

After about an hour-and-a-half of talking with Lauren, I'd had it. She was a disappointment, I was a disappointment, and the people I called my friends were disappointments.

It seemed everything around me was crashing. All of my idols, the things I had put my hope in, were letting me down. The girl I thought was the picture of perfection was dating some dirt-bag, was slinging dope, and throwing her life away. My friends were self-absorbed people who used me so that they could have a place to party. My family had a lot of issues going on that I wasn't comfortable talking to anyone about. Everything was falling apart.

Looking back, I can see how my emotions were way out of control. It would be easy to blame the alcohol for how I responded. I'm sure it had something to do with it, but the reality was I had been slowly unraveling emotionally and mentally for several years, and everything was about to come undone.

My anxiety and anger was through the roof, and I couldn't handle the stress. The people I asked to talk with me were too wrapped up in their own stuff and didn't have time for me. One kid was up in my bathroom throwing up, and tearing down the shower curtain. Other people were just doing whatever they felt like doing. No one cared, and I was sick of being there.

# CRASHING

I looked at Lauren in that moment, and said, "Well if you're going to kill yourself, then I'm going to beat you to it . . ."

I left that statement open ended. Half hoping it would shock her into turning her life around, but half hoping she'd understand my own desperation and rescue me from it.

**"If you are going to kill yourself, then I'm going to beat you to it."**

She tried to talk to me, but I jumped through a cloud of smoke on the back porch and ran in the back door of my parents' house. There were a few people in the kitchen, and they could tell I was upset.

From there, I went up the back staircase of the house and ran through the game room into my bedroom. Although we had collected everyone's keys, I knew where they were and easily grabbed the keys to my Camaro.

I ran down the front staircase, out the front door, and got into my car.

Turning the key, I heard the roar of the engine, and I revved it a few times. I locked the doors and began to pull away. As I was pulling away, my friend Mike came and sat down in front of my car while James was banging on the window telling me to get out. People were freaking out. The weird thing is that my

## SELF-DESTRUCTING

parents were home but no one tried to get them. Since it was after 1 AM, my friends didn't want to wake them up. Besides, they thought they had things under control.

After a minute or two, I turned the engine off, but kept the radio on. I had the band Rage Against the Machine blaring as the lyrics, "I won't do what you tell me…" rattled on and on and on. I was done. These people weren't my friends. My parents didn't care about me.

If there was a God, He was far, far away. Or so I thought.

I was bawling. I was tired of trying to live a life pleasing everyone only to have no one really pleased with me. I was tired of being used by my "friends." I was tired of feeling all alone, even when I was in a crowd. I was tired of trying to figure out if there was a God, and if there was, whether or not He cared for me. I was tired. I was angry. I was sad, depressed, and anxious.

The next thing that happened seemed strange to me for a moment. Some of my friends got into their cars and started moving them. At first, I wasn't sure what they were doing, but I quickly realized they were moving their cars so that I would be blocked in. I was trapped. Well, at least it appeared so at first.

All of a sudden, people started walking away from my car. I later found out that someone suggested that they should just leave me alone and let me cool off since I was blocked in and couldn't go anywhere. I truly believe my friends thought they were doing the best thing for me in that moment.

Sitting in my car alone, sweating, crying, and feeling like a trapped animal, I was looking for a way out. I looked left and realized there was enough space to go around the car in front of me if I could jump the curb. I would have just enough room between my car and the light post to get out and go. Who knows where I would go, but at this point my pride wouldn't let me concede to these people who suddenly had time for me, though earlier in the evening had been too busy with their own drama.

49

## TRAGEDY TO TRUTH

The following decisions will always haunt me.

I started my car again, put it into gear, hopped the curb to my left, went around the car in front of me, and sped to the end of the street. At the end of the street I ran the stop sign, turned right, and roared down the street. I approached the turn near the exit of my neighborhood. I tore around the corner and actually stopped at the stop sign.

I was idling in the left-hand lane, my adrenaline was pumping, my anxiety was through the roof, and I broke down sobbing and crying out to God.

If He was there, I didn't know it. I yelled, "Oh God, why?!" But there was no answer.

If I turned left, I could go through some back roads and head to the freeway. Again, I didn't know where to go, I just wanted to make a point, and maybe even scare some of my friends. I know I was being dramatic, but I wanted to be in control of my life.

Everything in my life had been chaos. For too long I had allowed the opinion of others to determine the decisions I made. For too long I had allowed my parents' approval to be the ultimate. One way or another, I was determined to break free from the emotional prison I found myself in.

I wanted to keep driving, but I suddenly had a strong urge to just go home, get out of the car, tell everyone to leave, and go to bed. Still very upset, I turned right onto the main street outside of my neighborhood. My car was loud, so the faster I went, the louder it got. I was flooring it, and by the time I was in third gear, I was flying through the neighborhood, close to 80 mph in a 35 mph zone.

As I went around a curve, I saw someone in the street with their arms up in the air, as if they were trying to get me to stop. My heart jumped with an unexpected shock, and I tried to swerve. It all happened too fast. He tried to jump out of the

## SELF-DESTRUCTING

way, but went the wrong direction. He rolled up the hood of my car, smashing through my windshield. He came through so hard and fast that it bent my steering wheel back towards me. My airbags deployed, and I lost control of the car. I went off the road, jumped a curb, drove over a tree, and then crashed to a stop between two other trees.

I later learned that the reason John was in the street at all was because Lauren had screamed, "Oh my God, he's going to kill himself!"

He was trying to stop me; to rescue me from what he believed was my own self-destruction. And I killed him.

# DISCUSSION QUESTIONS

1. Can you think of a time in your life when things seemed to be spinning out of control? What emotions did you feel? Where did you turn for help?

2. Who do you trust with the secrets of your heart, someone you can go to when everything seems to be blowing up in your face? Does this person just make you feel better, or do they take you to real hope in Jesus?

3. Casey mentions that his idols started crashing around him on that night. Why do you think he described girls, popularity, and fun as idols?

4. How close do you think you have come to totally self-destructing? Do you attribute your survival to God or luck? What do you think the Bible says about this?

5. When you read about Casey killing his friend, what emotions were you feeling? How would you feel if you were in Casey's position at that time?

## TRAGEDY TO TRUTH

6. If you close your eyes and imagine God watching the events of that night unfold, how do you think He felt? What does your response reveal concerning what He feels about you?

CHAPTER 8

# RECOVERY

John was a friend I had met in some classes, and he eventually became involved in the theatre department at school. He served in the crew and was very laid back. He liked to surf and had a great sense of humor. I just couldn't believe he was gone.

As I lay in my hospital bed, my world crashing around me at the news that I had killed John, I prayed "God take me instead of him, take me instead of him!" But that didn't happen.

I wanted to die so badly; if not of natural causes, then I'd figure out a way to do it myself. I looked at the IV positioned in the crease of my left arm. It hurt like crazy when I bent my arm, so I closed my arm hard hoping that it would kill me. It hurt badly, but I wasn't going to die from it. I'm not sure how resolved I was to actually kill myself, but I knew that I didn't want to live with the guilt of having killed my friend.

I lay in the hospital bed crying, dazed, and utterly defeated. I didn't deserve to live. If I killed my friend, then I deserved to die too. The fading thoughts of suicide that had haunted my past came roaring back.

## TRAGEDY TO TRUTH

My parents knew my history with anxiety and depression and were very concerned for me. They, too, were devastated by the loss of my friend and terrified that I wouldn't be able to handle the grief. They were worried I may try to take my own life, and with good reason.

Because of my unstable emotional history and my parents' concerns, I was taken to a mental hospital. The ride there was a blur, as was the intake process. Sitting in a wheelchair, still covered in glass and blood, they took a picture of me on a Polaroid for my file. Depressed, scared, hurt, and unsure of what I could and couldn't say due to legal ramifications, exhaustion began to cover me like a dark cloud. I needed sleep. I looked at the picture they had just taken of me and one word entered my mind; death. I looked like death in that picture. I had just seen death. I had just caused death. I felt dead.

After several hours, they finally took me to a room and let me take a shower. They placed a large male nurse outside of my bathroom door and made me keep the door cracked because I was on suicide watch. They were not going to let me have much privacy at all. As I stood leaning against the support rail on the shower wall, the warm water rinsed the glass and blood from my body. I was exhausted, devastated, and had very little desire to live. I needed help.

They finally let me go to bed later that afternoon. I awoke in the middle of the night to the sound of a girl screaming like a lunatic. I'm not sure what I expected, since I was in a mental hospital, but I was frightened by her screams and overwhelmed again by the gravity of what I had just done.

My parents came to see me in the hospital the next day. My dad was visibly concerned and angry with me, and my mom was just scared for what my life might become. By this time, I had concluded that I didn't want to hurt myself, especially because I didn't want to cause any further pain for my friends and family

## RECOVERY

than I already had. I was terrified that I would have to go to prison and didn't know what would happen next.

Over the next few days, my friends came to visit me. It was overwhelming how many of them showed up to visit. The hospital staff gave my visitors paper plates to write messages on for me, and I had people I hadn't talked to in some time come and visit. To be honest, it was a confusing time for me. Why didn't they all hate me for what I had done? Regardless, I remember feeling loved by them and felt like maybe we could actually get through this.

I received all sorts of religious trinkets and books from my visitors. I had a statue of Mary, a Rosary, a Bible, an AA Big Book, and all sorts of other confusing sentiments given to me. Needless to say, I was surrounded by a mixture of spirituality with no real grounding and with an uncertainty as to whether or not God even existed.

I was told that John's parents wanted to meet with me, and I was terrified. I hardly knew John's parents, and don't recall that I had ever actually met his dad before. But meeting John's parents was a pivotal point in my resolve to get well. They were surprisingly kind to me in spite of the fact that I was the cause of the death of their son.

As I was pushed into the dimly lit conference room, tears filled my eyes. The social worker stayed with me during our meeting, but I felt so alone, so exposed, and so broken. I kept apologizing, and they told me that they forgave me.

I remember very little about what was specifically said. However, I do remember they said to me, "John wouldn't want you to hurt yourself, and we don't want you to either."

His parents told me they were Christians and that they forgave me. They asked me if I had a relationship with Jesus. To be honest, I wasn't really sure what they meant, but I told them that I was a Christian. I believed that at the time, but looking

## TRAGEDY TO TRUTH

back I don't believe that I was. I had been to church before, I had said prayers, and read my Bible a few times, so I was sure that meant I was "in." I talked enough about church that they didn't push me too hard about being a Christian, but I could tell that they wanted me to know Jesus.

They proceeded to invite me to John's viewing and then to the funeral. The doctors discussed it and were convinced that I was not yet emotionally able to handle this kind of emotional stress. They compromised and said that I could pick which one I wanted to go to. So, I decided to go to his visitation, so that I could see him and say, "Goodbye."

After meeting with his parents, I was resolved to somehow find the strength to pull myself together and change my life. With the support of my family, friends, and John's family, I felt like I could do it.

I dreaded going to the visitation. I didn't want to see anyone. I didn't want to talk to anyone, and I didn't want to see him lying dead in a casket. I didn't wear slacks and a dress shirt often, but I remember being in front of the bathroom mirror getting dressed in my Sunday best and trying to do my hair. Looking in the mirror was difficult. I hated who I saw looking back at me.

My parents made arrangements for me to go to the funeral home early so I could have a few moments alone with John. As we arrived at the funeral home, my dad got my wheelchair out and wheeled me inside. The stench of the flowers was overwhelming, like they were trying to cover up death with the smell. The weight of the situation was brutal, and I was in tears immediately. A few people that I knew were already there to pay their respects, and they came up and hugged me and cried. I cried even harder, and wished they would leave me alone.

They pushed me into a small, dimly lit viewing room. To my right were a few rows of chairs for people to sit in, and

# RECOVERY

to my left was John's lifeless body in a casket. The casket was open, but a see-through purple lace was hung over the opening of the casket, apparently to keep people from putting anything in there. Surrounding the casket were several flower bouquets, pictures of John, and two surfboards.

John looked so peaceful, so quiet. It didn't look exactly like him, but he was easily recognizable. As I looked at him lying in that casket, it hit me like a ton of bricks. I did that. He was dead, and it was my fault. The reality was more than I could handle.

I asked my parents to take me back to the hospital, and they did. I went to bed early that night and woke early the next morning. While everyone was at the funeral, I was allowed to sit outside on the small porch at the end of our wing. I remember the sun was beaming down, and I had a sense of closure. Even though this sense of closure was momentary, it did solidify my desire to live and make the most out of my life. There was still a lot of uncertainty about what was to come, but I had to at least commit to doing my part in making my life different.

On Sunday morning, my parents went back to the United Methodist church that I had been confirmed in and met with the new pastor to tell him what had happened. They came to see me after church and told me that someone from the church would bring me communion. I wasn't really sure why I needed communion, but I thought it was a very kind gesture for them to reach out to me, especially after I had killed my friend.

Lisa, the lady who came to see me looked really familiar; perhaps I had known her several years before, during confirmation, or had seen her at the church. At any rate, it was nice to have someone from church whom I recognized. She didn't say very much, just that she was there to pray with me and to give me communion. I don't remember the prayer, but I remember the little bread-like wafer and the shot of grape juice, the kind we had when we were kids. It meant something

## TRAGEDY TO TRUTH

to me. Perhaps there was a God and maybe he might care about me, even after all I had done.

The new pastor, Marty, came to see me in the hospital the next day. We didn't visit for long, but I remember that he told me I had some important choices to make moving forward, about how I would live my life. If I'm not mistaken, he used a metaphor of being at a fork in the road and told me I needed to choose a path. He prayed for me and left.

After being in the mental hospital for five days, I was ready to get out. I felt like a mental patient and a prisoner, most certainly on lock down, but not yet arrested. I was still very scared about what I would have to face once I got out of the hospital, but was convinced that staying in the hospital long-term was not going to help my recovery.

After several days in the hospital, I sat in a meeting with my parents and a psychiatrist, begging them to let me go home. My parents were very reluctant to let me come home because of the trauma I had just endured and the amount of lying that I had done recently. I told them I would do whatever they told me to and that I would not be a problem, but that being in this place was not helping anymore.

They told me I had to go to physical therapy every morning and to psychological therapy every evening, and I would have to stay home and could only go places with them. Also, I promised to go to church and try to be more religious. I would have done anything they asked of me at that point, just so I could go home and get out of that horrible place.

Finally, the doctor, and I'd bet the insurance company, decided to release me from the hospital into my parents' care. I went home that evening, and shortly afterwards my friends came by to visit me. The initial conversations were pretty shallow, as they weren't really sure what to talk about or how to talk to me without talking about the elephant in the room.

RECOVERY

The first few days there were a lot of people at my house. They came and hung out with me. Some acted like nothing had happened, others were obviously conflicted on how they should feel about me. There were moments when I didn't think about what happened, but most of the time the crash haunted my every thought.

I didn't get much sleep because of my anxiety, the nightmares, and the flashbacks. So, I stayed up and wrote some bad poetry, tried to read the Bible, and thought about spiritual things. I also talked on the phone a lot. It was a hard place to be because no matter how many people were around, I still felt alone in my grief. I dreaded going back to school for my senior year, but it was closing in quickly.

# DISCUSSION QUESTIONS

1. Have you ever felt as alone and scared as you imagine Casey felt in the mental hospital? What brought about this loneliness in your life?

2. Are you surprised that John's parents were able to forgive Casey so quickly? Why do you think they could do this?

3. Pastor Marty told Casey he was at a fork in the road and had some important decisions to make about how he would live his life. Do you ever feel like this? What two roads are you facing?

4. How is the gospel displayed by the fact that God was pursuing Casey at this point in his life?

CHAPTER 9

# THE GRADUAL DECLINE

A year before my accident, there was a heavy rain in our area. Anne, a friend of mine, had gotten a ride home from Sean who was a friend of hers. Anne was always happy, bouncy, and full of energy. For some reason, she was always friendly to me, even when some of her friends didn't like me. Occasionally when she had friends spend the night, they'd sneak out of her house and come over to mine to hang out. I'm not sure how we met, but I really cared a lot about her. The night of the storm, Sean was driving a small sports car at a very high speed. He lost control and slammed into a telephone pole on the passenger side, where Anne was sitting. She was killed instantly.

I remember I pulled into my driveway and my girlfriend, Kristie, pulled up and told me there had been a bad crash, and she'd heard it was Anne. I jumped into her car, and we drove around the corner to the crash scene. The roads were blocked off, but I remember seeing the little red car with a tarp over it, wrapped around the telephone pole. Whoever it was, there wasn't much hope for them.

## TRAGEDY TO TRUTH

We found out an hour or two later that it was indeed Anne, and she was killed immediately. Sean, the guy driving the car, was in a coma in the hospital, and they weren't sure if he'd make it either. I was so upset, angry, and I felt so helpless. At that point in my life, I doubted that there was even a God, but I still remained a nominal agnostic, just in case that counted for something.

The next day we went to Anne's parents' house to give our condolences and to mourn together. I had never met her family before, but they were very sweet people. Her older brother came in and spoke some reason to us, angry and hurting teenagers. He said, "It could have happened to any of us. All of us have been guilty of speeding at one time or another."

That was a sobering statement, because I knew it was true of me. It also defused my angry feelings towards Sean. However, there were some people who felt nothing but rage and hatred towards him. The rest of his time in high school was very rough. People said the most horrible things, both to his face and behind his back. Old friends called him a 'murderer' and other awful things. He wasn't a murderer. He was a foolish teenager who'd made a bad choice with horrendous consequences.

There was a visitation the night before Anne's funeral, and I remember going in the funeral home and walking up to the casket. It was heartbreaking to see her broken, delicate, and dead body lying in the casket, knowing that she would never smile or laugh with me again. She was dead and she wasn't coming back.

The next day, the funeral home's chapel was packed with people who were crying, and shocked. It was the first time many of them had ever experienced loss, and they were trying to make sense of all that they were feeling and experiencing. I had lost friends and family members before, so it wasn't as shocking for me. However, it was very sad and left me asking a lot of deeper questions about the meaning of life, and whether or not there

62

was a God who cared for us. I couldn't understand why a loving God would allow something like this to happen to such a sweet girl. It just didn't make sense.

One year later, and for very different reasons, I found myself in Sean's shoes, fearing what people would say, what my friends would say, and how my last year of high school would play out.

# THE FIRST DAY OF SCHOOL

My long-term girlfriend, Kristie, and I got back together a few weeks after the crash, and she gave me a ride to school the first day of our senior year. I was very nervous to go back to school because I assumed people had been talking about me since the crash, much like they had been hateful toward Sean the year before.

Still trying to make sense of my own nightmare, I walked into school and saw some of the friends who had been hanging out with me during the summer after my crash. At this point they were all still being very supportive. However, people that I had known and partied with, but who I was not close to, were obviously uncomfortable around me.

Looking back, I understand why it was weird for them to be around me. After all, I had killed one of our friends, and what do you really say about that? Some people didn't want to say the wrong thing, others didn't know what to say, and still others had nothing nice to say but lacked the courage to say it to my face.

I had to go see my psychologist almost every day after school. We sat and talked about the crash, but I wasn't allowed to share many details because my psychologist could possibly be called to testify against me in court. This made it very difficult to really work through much of the actual incident, but it was helpful to talk about friendships and relationships, especially

# TRAGEDY TO TRUTH

over the course of the coming weeks and months, as many of the relationships I still had would fall apart.

Oddly enough, the State's blood-alcohol test came back below the level of intoxication, and they gave me my license back. At first, my parents were hesitant to allow me to drive again, and rightly so. However, over the next few weeks my parents made the decision to get me a Ford Explorer so that I could drive to and from school.

I definitely did not expect the backlash this caused among my friends at school.

My parents picked me up from school in my new car and let me drive home. I saw my girlfriend in the parking lot and stopped to talk to her, showing her my new car. She looked stunned rather than happy for me. I didn't understand what the problem was. She called me that night and broke up with me.

Perhaps on some level my friends saw this as me moving on, callously forgetting (as if I ever could) the death I had caused with my previous vehicle.

## AN OUTCAST

It wasn't long before my friends at school became very cold and short with me. The day after I got my new car (and the day after Kristie had broken up with me), I wasn't sure who to sit with at lunch. I suddenly felt unwelcome with anyone I considered a friend, soI ended up sitting out in a courtyard with some kids a few years younger than me. Most of them were aspiring to be in rock bands, and since I had played in one, they let me hang out. Also, most of them were very aware of what it was like to be an outcast, so they didn't mind being seen with me.

I was so lonely and didn't feel like I had any friends left. When I got my new vehicle it made people think that I didn't care about what I had done, that it didn't bother me, and that I

64

# THE GRADUAL DECLINE

wasn't sorry. This couldn't have been further from the truth, and I resented them for seeming to care about me so much and then in an instant changing and treating me like an enemy.

My friend, JR, invited me to eat lunch with him and two of his friends. While I was grateful for the rockers welcoming me to their lunch table, I was starved to have some more meaningful conversations. When I went out into the smaller courtyard with JR, I saw that he was eating lunch with two girls his age. One was this cute little redhead named Stephanie. I had met her briefly the year before and knew who she was, but I didn't know her very well. The other girl was named Karyn, and she and Steph were very kind to me. From then on, we began eating lunch together every day. It was a brief break from the stress and loneliness that I was experiencing during my senior year of high school.

At the end of that month, my grandfather, George, had a sudden stroke and died. I missed a few days of school to attend his funeral and to spend time with family. While I was out, a lot of the students talked with our theater teacher, about me and the crash a conversation which resulted in a large group of them being pulled out of class to meet and talk about it all. They felt like I didn't care, that I wasn't sorry, and that I had no regrets about what I had done. I'm sure the school felt like this was helpful in giving them a place to process their grief, but for me, it felt like betrayal.

I was so devastated by their actions. In a matter of less than two months I had been in the crash, broken up with a long-term girlfriend, and lost my grandfather. Now all of my 'friends' were talking behind my back and saying things that were just not true.

When my parents found out about this meeting they were understandably upset. I was hurt and felt betrayed by people who had been my best friends. My teacher said I could address

## TRAGEDY TO TRUTH

the class, so I got up and told them that I wasn't allowed to talk about the details of the crash but that I was very sorry, and that if they had any questions or concerns that they could come and talk to me directly.

Over the course of the first few months of school, I went from having a solid group of friends, to no friends, to a new group of younger friends.

One of the ways God showed His kindness to me during this time was to bring Steph into my life. She was two years younger, but she was mature for her age in many ways. We began talking on the phone everyday and had a great time laughing and joking around, though her parents were wary of me and for good reason. When I asked her to go out with me, her parents said that she could not go anywhere with me but agreed to let me visit her at their house. I'm sure her parents thought this would deter me and that I'd move on, however, I really liked this girl, and seeing as how I didn't have many other friends, I agreed to their terms.

I still remember the first time I went to their house. Her dad was a cop, so I was extra nervous to meet him. I took out my hoop earrings and put in some studs so I would look more conservative. Surprisingly, her parents were very kind and welcoming to me. I could tell they weren't sure what to make of me at first, but the more I came around, the more they seemed to warm up to me.

After a few weeks, Steph was allowed to go out with me in a group of friends, and then she was finally able to ride with me for homecoming. As all of my old friendships collapsed, a new relationship began to form that seemed to have a lot of promise. Unfortunately, I had a lot of emotional baggage from the crash and from several other unhealthy relationships, so I brought a good share of problems and sin into this relationship.

**THE GRADUAL DECLINE**

# DISCUSSION QUESTIONS

1. Of all the emotional responses people had toward Casey after his crash, which do you think you would have had? Why?

2. Have you ever experienced the conditional love that Casey felt from people who turned against him? How is this different from the love God shows us?

3. When you make a mistake or commit a sin, how do you think God feels about you? How does this line up with what Scripture says?

CHAPTER 10

# CONVERSION

"And I am sure of this, that he who began a good work in you will bring it to completion at the day of Jesus Christ." Apostle Paul, Philippians 1:6 (ESV)

Becoming a Christian is difficult for someone who already thinks they are one. Since I had gone to church off-and-on growing up, and I was raised in a "Christian" family, I figured that I was a Christian. I prayed, went to church, sang the songs, and for the most part was a fairly 'good' person, so I figured that things were set. But, for a few years leading up to the crash and the time immediately following it, I had begun to seriously question whether or not the Christian religion was even true.

The Christians that I knew were either hypocritical, meaning they went to church but did all of the bad stuff that I did, or they were super uptight and judgmental. Either way, if their faith made a difference at all, then it was too small to interest me. To be involved in a religion that made no difference, or a negative difference, was a huge waste of time.

After the crash, several people gave me Bibles and religious literature. My mom bought me a cross and a Bible for teenagers.

## TRAGEDY TO TRUTH

I began wearing the cross immediately, mostly as a good luck charm, but the Bible I didn't really use very often. I tried to read it, but since I didn't like reading, and had no idea where to start, I mostly only turned to it when sadness, depression, and loneliness got the best of me. Even then, most of what I read didn't make sense to me.

My pride prevented me from asking for help. If I'd asked what to read, or how to read the Bible, then people might realize I wasn't a Christian after all. To be honest, my whole conversion process was messy. On the one hand, I thought that if there was a God, He would not accept me because of what I had done. On the other hand, I was prideful and thought that I wasn't 'that' bad. Even though I had caused a crash that resulted in the death of my friend, I had not intended on hurting anyone. I constantly bounced back and forth between self-inflicting condemnation and false hope in my good behavior.

This type of inconsistent spiritual faith was disappointing. To hope in my ability to perform or behave quickly became tiresome. I was confused, but too concerned about what other people thought about me to ask anyone for help. I wasn't sure whom I would ask anyway. Going to church only taught me about Christian rituals and that some people seemed to believe in Jesus, at least enough to dress up for him on Sundays.

The quest to be religious was so frustrating, but despite my frustration, there seemed to be something that constantly pulled me back to thinking about this Jesus I read about in my Bible.

Could God really become man, live a perfect life, and die a gruesome death, only to be raised from the dead? Could God really raise Jesus from the dead? Why was this important? How could this, if true, help me? Was there more to believing in Jesus than just being a nice person, staying away from sin, and going to church? These were some of the questions that were constantly

CONVERSION

stirring in my head. The major problem was that I didn't know where to find the answers, and I refused to ask for help.

Then one night during the spring of my senior year of high school, the church was having a revival-type weekend. They brought in a speaker from Tennessee. He was an African American United Methodist Preacher. I always think its funny to watch black preachers in white churches. White people aren't sure how to act and the preachers help them along and encourage them to 'talk back' and say "Amen". The white people sure do try, but it is still hilarious to watch them.

Although I didn't know much about the Bible, I remember that this man was talking about a paralyzed guy that Jesus healed. I later learned that it was from the Gospel of John in the fifth chapter. Jesus found this guy lying by a pool of water who had been paralyzed for a long time. The myth about the pool was that when the water was stirred, whoever could get into the water first would be healed. This would be a tough feat for a paralyzed guy. No way HE was getting in first, for sure.

# DO YOU WANT TO BE WELL?

Jesus asked this guy a question that seemed very weird. He asked, "Do you want to be well?" The man said that he did, but began making excuses about why he couldn't get into the water. Jesus then healed him on the spot. I remember like it was yesterday, the preacher looking at the crowd and asking, "Do you want to be well?"

Something happened inside me the moment he asked that question.

I had been paralyzed all of my life by fear, by depression, by tragedy, by pride, and always had an excuse for why I did what I did. I even had good reason for my sin. He cut through all of that by repeating the question that Jesus asked the man,

TRAGEDY TO TRUTH

and I remember vividly thinking to myself, "If Jesus will heal me, I want to be well."

Like I said, my conversion was messy.

The preacher asked people to come forward to pray, but I stayed in my chair. I sat in my chair wondering what to do next. Would Jesus really make me well? Would he accept me? I didn't pray any special prayers that night, but I did ask Jesus to make me well.

In that moment, with that heartfelt plea, "Jesus will you make me well?" I realized the saving grace of Jesus Christ and my need for Him to save me.

It wasn't the way it normally happened, at least not in the churched world, but nonetheless, it was genuine and honest. I had officially asked Jesus to save me, heal me, and make me whole.

Still, I had a long way to go.

# FREE AT LAST

My theology (knowledge of God) at the time was more of a Me-ology (knowledge of myself and my way of thinking projected onto God). Instead of understanding that I was created in God's image, I was busy creating God in my image.

Early on I thought I could live for God only when it was convenient, but as it turned out, God wanted all of me. My life was no longer my own. I belonged to Him, 100%, and that was how much of me He wanted me to surrender to Him. (1 Corinthians 6:19-20).

Over the course of the next few years, with the help of some people God placed in my life, I began to realize that I was forgiven of my sins because of what Jesus has accomplished on the cross, and I was also called to live for Him.

Still, doubt was a constant enemy of my faith in those early years. There were days when I woke up and thought, "Do I even

CONVERSION

believe all of this?" I had a ton of questions and a lot of doubt, but I didn't know who to bother with it all. Fortunately, over the years, God placed certain men in my life, men who taught me that growing in Christ meant that doubts would come. Men who taught me that God gave us His Word, His Spirit, and His people, the church to help us overcome those doubts. Without God, His people, and His Word, my faith would have been gone for sure.

On my own, I did not have the strength to maintain faithfulness to Him, but by His strength all things were and are made possible.

Being rescued by Jesus slowly began to change everything in my life. I was able to face the consequences for the crash with courage. I stood in front of other teenagers talking to them about the importance of making good choices and the dangers of drinking and driving, and most importantly, I found hope in the fact that I had been forgiven by the God who made me.

My conversion was a true transformation. I was, at last, free.

# DISCUSSION QUESTIONS

1. Do you believe you are a Christian? If so, what is this belief based on? Does the Bible support your belief?

2. What is the difference between religion and following Jesus? Which one do you feel more comfortable with?

3. If you went to church and saw someone who had done something like Casey did, how do you honestly think you would feel in your heart towards them? How do you think your honest answer lines up with the gospel?

4. Do you identify more with the offender (Casey) or the offended (John's family and friends) as you read this story? Why do you feel this way?

# PART II
# TRUTH

CHAPTER 11

# CONSEQUENCES

I didn't grow up learning how to take responsibility for my actions. Perhaps because my dad is a great lawyer and taught me how to argue my way past any wrongdoings; or because my mom often made excuses for my behavior, trying to soften the stern military-style relationship I had with my dad. Or maybe, I didn't take responsibility for my actions because I was incredibly good at reading people and then manipulating them for my own gain.

Whatever the reason, from a young age, I learned to make excuses for my behavior or blame someone else for something that was my fault. I hid and blame-shifted, much like Adam did in Genesis 3:8-12.

When Adam was confronted by God for sinning, he was hiding from Him. When Adam spoke to God, he blamed Eve and didn't take any responsibility for what he had done.

And they heard the sound of the LORD God walking in the garden in the cool of the day, and the man and his wife hid themselves from the presence of the LORD God among the trees of the garden. ⁹ But the LORD God called to the man and said to

# TRAGEDY TO TRUTH

him, *"Where are you?"*[10] And he said, *"I heard the sound of you in the garden, and I was afraid, because I was naked, and I hid myself."*[11] He said, *"Who told you that you were naked? Have you eaten of the tree of which I commanded you not to eat?"*[12] The man said, *"The woman whom you gave to be with me, she gave me fruit of the tree, and I ate."* Genesis 3:8-12

In the same way, taking responsibility for my actions was not something I was accustomed to, and it did not come easily. A few days after graduating from high school, I appeared in court to face the legal consequences for the crash. It had been eleven months since the accident and there were several different charges floating around during that time. At one time, they talked about charging me with Intoxicated Manslaughter, which was a 2nd degree felony. I likely would have served time in prison. However, the official blood test taken by the state somehow came back under the legal level of intoxication. Also, my friend's parents were gracious and told the district attorney that they thought I could do more outside of jail than I could inside.

My attorney finally made a deal with the district attorney, which placed me on probation for five years. During that time, I had to complete 200 hours of community service and have a breathalyzer in my car at all times. However, before my deal with the DA could be finalized, I had to go to court and appear before a judge. The days leading up to this were very difficult because I feared the judge would decide not to accept the deal. It was completely out of my hands.

I woke up the morning I was to be in court, put on a stiff shirt and tie, and rode with my parents to court. I was nervous, feeling like I could throw up any moment. I didn't want to go to court. I felt like I had been punished enough with the nightmares, flashbacks, and the loss of my friends, but I knew that it was time to face the consequences for my actions like a man.

# CONSEQUENCES

The courtroom was old and smelled like an antique shop mixed with wood polish. John's parents were there, wearing pins with a picture of their son on them. They did not speak to me or even look my direction, so I silently went with my attorney to the table. When things got started, I was asked to stand by the judge. He gave me a brief lecture and then asked me if I understood the charges, and what my deal with the DA meant.

I told him through tears that I did. My attorney asked if I could spend some of my community service hours speaking to teenagers about the dangers of drinking and driving and the importance of making good choices. He said that I could spend 10% of my 200 hours speaking and the rest would have to be done through the community service department for the county.

After the judge hit his gavel, we signed some papers and were dismissed. There was a reporter from the Houston Chronicle there writing about the story. Other than her and a few other people, the courtroom was relatively empty. She asked me a few brief questions and then we left. We headed a few miles down the road and went to the probation department to register and to fill out paperwork. It was a very long and draining day.

After a long wait, I was finally called back and they took a picture of me, a mug shot. Since I was hospitalized after the accident and never formally arrested, I had to be fingerprinted as well. I told my probation officer I had already been making changes, and I wouldn't be a problem. I'm sure he had heard this hundreds of times before, and I knew that I would have to spend the next five years proving that I was different.

The next morning, my parents woke me up to show me an article about my story in the Houston Chronicle. We began getting invitations that day for me to come and speak for various groups in and around the Houston area. There was one big problem; I had only a few weeks until my first talk, and I didn't know what I was going to say!

## TRAGEDY TO TRUTH

The first talk was at a driving school nearby for the students. I took Steph with me and went into the brightly lit room. I had a few pictures of my wrecked Camaro and had them blown up pretty large to use as an illustration for my story. I was anxious about sharing, and it was hard to relive the incident. I was involved in theater throughout high school, so I was used to being on a stage as a character. However, standing in front of thirty of my peers at a Drivers Education class proved to be daunting. I don't remember exactly what I said. I'm sure it was scattered, but I made it through.

Some of the kids came up to me afterwards and thanked me for sharing, but I could tell that some of the kids were judging me. Well, I don't know for sure if they were judging me, but it felt like it. I would've judged me if I had been one of those students. I'm sure some of them thought I was a criminal and that I wasn't worth listening to. However, I was convinced if I could help just a few of these kids keep from making the same mistakes that I had, then it might be worth experiencing the judgment of the others.

I enjoyed speaking because it helped me connect with a lot of students. The rest of my community service was working in the Literacy Lab for the probation department. It was weird being eighteen years old and having to tutor people in their fifties who were on probation for felonies. They were required to pursue a GED while on probation and had to come to this lab. Needless to say, not many of them wanted to be there. One guy came in drunk all of the time. I'm not sure how he was never busted, but all he'd do is play the beginning reading games and mouth off. In fact, I got into some trouble once when I shared my story to people in the lab. I'm thinking the drunk guy didn't like what I had to say.

Oddly enough, while I was working towards completing my hours and speaking to students, there were times when I struggled

## CONSEQUENCES

to take full ownership and responsibility for what I had done. The big hang up for me was that I never intended to hurt anyone, and now I was being treated like a killer. I was told that I likely wouldn't even be on probation if I hadn't been drinking on the night of the crash. However, here I was, a criminal on probation.

Over the course of several years in counseling and growing in my faith in Jesus, I came to learn that taking responsibility isn't a path to bondage, but the path to freedom. When I began to face my consequences as graces rather than punishment, I learned that this season of life could be corrective and transformative.

Ultimately, Jesus took the ultimate consequence for our sin on the cross. Becoming the perfect sacrifice, He took our punishment, which was a death sentence, in order that we might have life forever with Him. With that in mind, I began to press into the consequences and face them head on, rather than making excuses for why I did what I did. In this, there was true freedom.

## DISCUSSION QUESTIONS:

1. Have you ever had a hard time taking responsibility for your actions? What made it so difficult?

2. In what ways can we experience God's grace through the consequences we face for our actions?

3. Is there anything in your past that you know you should take responsibility for that you have avoided doing so? If so, what is it and why do you think you've avoided that responsibility?

4. How can we grow through the consequences for our actions moving forward?

5. How can we encourage others to grow through the consequences they face?

CHAPTER 12

# ANXIETY AND DEPRESSION

There is no way to adequately describe what living your entire life under the cloud of anxiety and depression feels like. If you've lived that life, then you know what I mean, but if you haven't, well, then you're just going to have to take my word for it; it's overwhelming and crushing and requires most of your effort, some days, just to breathe.

And when I say your "entire life" I literally mean your. entire. life.

As far back as I can remember, I was an anxious and worried little kid. If my parents argued, I felt nervous. If my sister was upset, then I was upset. If my mom seemed worried, I felt worried. If a friend was sad, I was sad. When a teacher was mad at another student, I was somehow at fault. Whatever those around me were feeling, I felt too.

And as I mentioned before, I worried obsessively about things, not things *likely* to occur, mind you, but things that haunted me as if they were not only likely, but impending.

83

TRAGEDY TO TRUTH

I hated feeling out of control, and anxious and worried, but those emotions were a part of my daily life.

Eventually the constant barrage of anxiety wore me down and led to depression. My psychological issues started causing physical problems, and to their credit, my parents sought professional help for me.

According to the National Institute for Mental Health, about 11 percent of adolescents have a depressive disorder by age 18. And according to the World Health Organization, major depressive disorder is the leading cause of disability among Americans among 18-44 year olds. These are real statistics, based on actual case studies from decades of research.[i]

I am giving you these statistics because I do not want to minimize the reality of mental illness. Nor do I want to suggest that seeking professional help from a psychologist, psychiatrist, or other forms of medical intervention are unnecessary or unhelpful.

And, because I have shared this story for many years, I know that most of you reading this are either young males, or the parent of a child or teen struggling with many of the same things I struggled with throughout my childhood and adolescence.

I don't want to minimize the struggle you are experiencing, or the fact that you are searching for real answers.

What I want to do is share with you the hope and the eventual freedom that I experienced.

## A SEARCH FOR SOMETHING BETTER

From elementary school through college I saw multiple psychologists, psychotherapists, and psychiatrists. And while they offered some help, it was all pretty temporary. The primary issue

---

[i] *http://www.nimh.nih.gov/statistics/1MDD_CHILD.shtml*

## ANXIETY AND DEPRESSION

was that their approach was to focus on myself, improving myself, being at peace with myself, and looking out for myself. The result was often more harmful than helpful, because the more I became aware of myself, the more aware I was of my faults, my insecurities and my selfishness.

What was intended to help me, ultimately led me to fluctuate between self-reliance and deep despair.

## THE CRAZY CYCLE OF WORRY

Just worry, worry, worry. I've struggled on and off with anxiety and depression since I was six years old. I became a Christian when I was seventeen. I'm in my thirties now, and I still struggle with those things at times.

There is a pattern I fall into again and again. It's a crazy cycle. A hamster wheel that gets me nowhere, but for some reason, I jump on it anyway.

I get anxious. I get obsessive about my anxiety. I continue to be anxious. Biologically, it depletes the chemicals I need, and I become clinically depressed. It happens differently for different people. We can't lie to ourselves and say anxiety only affects us spiritually, or it only affects us emotionally. It also affects us physically.

I'm not trying to come up0 with a self-help way to make you better. I'm exposing the fact that when you worry, **you have a good reason to worry, because you're relying on yourself and YOU simply cannot help yourself.**

## BUT THERE IS HOPE

One of the greatest passages dealing with how the truth of God's Word transforms our anxiety is found in Philippians 4 in the New Testament. The verses found in Philippians 4:6-7 are very dear to my heart.

*"Don't fret or worry. Instead of worrying, pray.
Let petitions and praises shape your worries
into prayers, letting God know your concerns.
Before you know it, a sense of God's wholeness,
everything coming together for good, will
come and settle you down. It's wonderful what
happens when Christ displaces worry at the
center of your life." Philippians 4:6-7 MSG*

Some of my most frequent sins, sins I still struggle with today, are anxiety, worry, and trying to be in control of what can happen tomorrow while missing out on what God has for me today. I think one of the greatest ways that I become ineffective for Kingdom work is by being wrapped up in all my worries.

- What's going to happen?
- How are we going to make it?
- How are we going to pay our bills?
- What are we going to do?

## SHIFTING THE WAY YOU THINK

In Philippians, Paul tells us to shift the way we think. Part of worship is changing the way we view God, and the way we view ourselves. If you are relying on yourself or someone else besides God to make your situation better, you're in trouble, because it's never going to work. I know this, firsthand.

Philippians 4:4-7 says,

Rejoice in the Lord always; again I will say, rejoice. Let your reasonableness be known to everyone. The Lord is at hand; do not be anxious about anything, but in everything by

## ANXIETY AND DEPRESSION

prayer and supplication with thanksgiving let your requests be made known to God. And the peace of God, which surpasses all understanding, will guard your hearts and your minds in Christ Jesus.

He says twice to "Rejoice in the Lord."

Find your joy, your happiness, your satisfaction in the Lord. Again, I go back to the Gospel I explained earlier. The joy we have is in the fact that when we are helpless, God is our helper. When we are spiritually sick, he makes us well. When we are spiritually dead, he gives us life. Rejoice in the one who rescues you, saves you, brings you hope, and gives you this eternal promise of forever with him. He is the one who enables you to lift your eyes from your current situation and place your hope in the one who will return, redeem, judge, and make all things new.

But if God is going to be the most satisfying thing in your life, if you are going to truly rejoice in Him, then you are going to have to get to know Him better. Unless you have a deeper, consequential understanding of who God is, the nature of God, then it's going to be really difficult to find joy in God. That takes time. It takes intentionality. It takes effort.

When I tell people to spend time in the Bible, it's not just so they can become more knowledgeable. That will most likely just produce spiritual arrogance and not real life change, and we both know plenty of people like that. Don't be those people. No, when I tell people to read the Bible, it's so they can get to know the God whose words are found there.

When Paul exhorts us to "Rejoice in the Lord," he means living with an attitude that says, "God, even if I don't see how you're working this situation, I trust you. I trust that you're good. I trust that you're sovereign. I trust that you bring redemption. I trust that you control all things and work good in all things for those who love you and are called according to your purpose."

And the only way you're going to be able to trust God is to know Him, intimately.

# DO NOT BE ANXIOUS

Philippians 4:6 says, *"Do not be anxious about anything, but in everything by prayer and supplication with thanksgiving let your requests be made known to God." * Look at that again. *"Don't be anxious about anything, but in everything . . ."*

If you have your Bible with you and you have a pen, underline that. Are you ever anxious about anything?

Now look at the command of Jesus in Matthew 6:34:

> *"Give your entire attention to what God is doing right now, and don't get worked up about what may or may not happen tomorrow. God will help you deal with whatever hard things come up when the time comes."*

Jesus says not to worry about tomorrow, for tomorrow has enough struggles of its own. Rather, be concerned with what's going on today, what's going on right now. It's a command against helplessly existing and fostering anxiety. Constantly worrying about tomorrow and all that "might" happen is destructive and will tear you apart.

I know the hardest thing to do when your life feels out of control is to relinquish or give up control. In fact, for most of us, the more out of control our lives feel, the tighter we hold on. But let's face it; white-knuckling it has gotten us nowhere. And giving up control is exactly what Jesus is telling us to do in this passage. He's telling us to willingly give up control to God and

## ANXIETY AND DEPRESSION

trust Him in the right now of this moment AND in what will happen tomorrow.

Easy to say? Yep.

Easy to do? Not so much.

# THE SIN OF ANXIETY

Anxiety is a sin, and as much as Christians and non-Christians alike hate the word sin, it's an important word for us to understand.

Sin is something that separates us from God. It makes the divide between Him and us wider. The more we sin, the wider the gap. The wider the gap, the less we hear Him calling to us, the less we feel him reaching out to us, until eventually the sound and the impact of the worry in our lives overwhelms us.

Anxiety is a sin. It is our way of saying that we cannot trust God, that He cannot fix our problems, and that He doesn't care about us. It's the sin of unbelief, and also one of the greatest ways Satan convinces us to doubt God.

I've had clinical anxiety, so I know it's overwhelming. And early on in my faith I gave prayer and God about a two-minute shot, but here's what I can tell you now.

**We need to trust God because we CAN trust Him.**

That said, when I am in the midst of struggling with something and someone tells me "you just need to trust God, I want to slap them-metaphorically speaking, of course (well, sometimes for real).

"Oh, you just need to trust God. You just need to trust God. You need to trust Jesus with that. Trust the Lord with that." If we're having a stop and chat at the grocery store and you say, "We need to trust God," fine. But, if I'm sitting with you at dinner and I'm telling you about all of the struggles in my life, and your response is something like, "Well, just trust Jesus."

89

Those are not words of love. Those are not words of comfort. It's not helpful. I already KNOW I need to trust God. I need to know HOW to trust God.

Fortunately, Paul doesn't just throw out an abstract idea, "Well, just trust Jesus."

*"Do not be anxious about anything, but in everything by prayer and supplication with thanksgiving let your requests be made known to God."*

Instead, he says, "Here is how to trust God."

## PRAY

"Here is how to trust. We pray." That means we communicate with God, not just talking like God's a drive-through miracle machine, but listening. We listen.

And we ask (Paul says, "with prayer and supplication). Supplication means that we ask or we beg for something earnestly and humbly. "God, you're the only one who can do this. You're the only one who can provide. You're in control of all things."

We go to God and ask Him.

## BE HUMBLE

When we focus on God and take joy in Him, even when we don't feel it, He's faithful to us. We ask for what we need, and we do it humbly. We don't bark at God like those people on TV who tell God what to do in Jesus' name. That's superstition, not faith.

God is not your voodoo doll, and He's not some genie who will do what you want if you yell out or rub the lamp long enough. God exists to glorify himself by taking care of us, providing for us, and saving us. We have to be careful how we take our requests to God. We beg with a humble attitude. We go with the attitude that God is God, and we are not. We communicate with God and we ask for what we need.

ANXIETY AND DEPRESSION

# BE THANKFUL

Here is the unique, crazy part; we are to pray with a thankful heart. But that seems like a crazy request when we are

- anxious (obviously, not focused on being thankful in this moment)
- angry
- uncomfortable
- frustrated

When we pray with thanksgiving, it means we are trusting in God's goodness and His faithfulness, reflecting on all that He has done and has promised to do. It's shifting our focus from our situation (which, let's face it, if we're in charge of fixing, is hopeless) to the one who's actually able to do something about it.

You show gratitude for what He has already done in your life. Look, He has already given you and me, (if we're believers in Christ), way more than we deserve.

Let me throw this out there. Anything that happens that's bad, we deserve worse. Anything that happens that's great, that's a gift. It's grace. That's not fun to say. That's not a warm, fuzzy statement. To be honest with you, it's way easier just to say, "oh you don't deserve this struggle in your life." But the truth is we deserve hell and God has given us heaven. I'd say that deserves some thanksgiving.

# MY PRAYERS OF GRATITUDE

In these circumstances, we give thanks by saying, "God, thank you for saving us. Thank you that this is not our home. Thank you that we have redemption in Christ. Thank you that you don't hold our past against us, the wrongs others committed against us. You see us pure and clean, washed as white as snow,

## TRAGEDY TO TRUTH

because of Jesus Christ. Thank you for hearing my prayers. Thank you that you can change us. Thank you that you're a God who performs miracles. Thank you that you're a God who is in control. Thank you that you're a God who is faithful, even when we're faithless."

This attitude of thanksgiving is necessary.

Are there days when I'm tempted to not be thankful? Yes, of course.

Am I riding that? No.

Gratitude is the one thing that helps me find satisfaction in God.

And I'll be honest. Sometimes when I am overcome with anxiousness, and I pray with gratitude, I feel kind of fake, but I know in my mind and my heart that this keeps me coming back to God. When I struggle with anxiety, it reminds me that God is in control.

So, when I struggle, I pray these prayers of gratitude. And when you struggle, you can pray these prayers as well, until your own prayers of gratitude find their way into your heart and mind.

Anxiety is now an opportunity for God to woo me to Himself. When things are going well and I'm feeling self-reliant, when things are going well and I've got great friends around me, when my family is doing well and my life feels calm, I'm thankful.

When things feel out of control, my anxiety is ramped up and it reminds me of my great desperation for God. In those times, I need to go to God in prayer, with supplication and thanksgiving.

When our anxiety is hitting us hard, God is in control. He answers our prayers the way He needs to. Why? For His reputation. If he valued you or me higher than Himself, He'd no longer be fit to be God. He'd be an idol worshipper. He'd worship someone or something more than He worships Himself. He's the ultimate. He's supreme. Because of that, we can hope

## ANXIETY AND DEPRESSION

and trust in Him. He's not going to deny Himself, and that's good news.

His worth and value as God are not diminished when we mess up. He continues in His faithfulness. He answers prayers according to His will and for your good, even if you don't see it right now. Here's the promise, and this is a good promise.

Philippians 4:7 says, "And the peace of God, which surpasses all understanding, will guard your hearts and your minds in Christ Jesus." "The peace of God." What does this "peace of God" do? It guards, protects, shelters your minds, which anxiety is prone to conquer and take over. When we take our requests to God we are, once again, placing our trust in Him. Therefore, we can rest in peace.

Placing your trust in Christ, especially when you're anxious, sets your hope, not in the unknown, but in the One who knows all.

That's where we find rest. That's where we find this peace. It's not manifested in our own ability to control and correct our lives. The more you labor to know Him, the more you labor to have intimacy with Him, the more joy and satisfaction is experienced.

# REAL-LIFE APPLICATION

Philippians 4:8-9 says, "Finally, brothers, whatever is true, whatever is honorable, whatever is just, whatever is pure, whatever is lovely, whatever is commendable, if there is any excellence, if there is anything worthy of praise, think about these things. What you have learned and received and heard and seen in me—practice these things, and the God of peace will be with you." He tells us how we can find peace, and this peace will guard our minds and our hearts when we take our needs to God, thanking Him for who He is and shifting our focus out of our situation and towards Jesus.

# TRAGEDY TO TRUTH

The question arises, "If I'm not going to think about the things that worry me, what should I consume myself thinking about?" I want to show you something in Matthew 12:43-45. Jesus gives this illustration; "When the unclean spirit has gone out of a person, it passes through waterless places seeking rest, but finds none. Then it says, 'I will return to my house from which I came.' And when it comes, it finds the house empty, swept, and put in order. Then it goes and brings with it seven other spirits more evil than itself, and they enter and dwell there, and the last state of that person is worse than the first. So also will it be with this evil generation."

Jesus is saying when we go and dump our needs, gratitude, and requests on God, but we don't fill our minds intentionally with something else, the worry will just come back worse. Paul helps us in Philippians 4:8 to know what we should think about. What should we think about? Well, we should think about what is true, think about things that are honorable, things that are just, things that are pure, things that are lovely, things that are commendable, things that are excellent, things that are worthy of praise.

## ANSWER THESE QUESTIONS:

1. **What is true?**

   What are some things that are true?


2. **What is honorable?**

   What are things that are honorable that you can remind yourself of, even in the midst of anxiety?

## ANXIETY AND DEPRESSION

### 3. What is worthy of praise?

What are some testimonies of people in your life who have been radically changed by the Gospel of Jesus Christ, who struggled with infertility but God blessed them with a baby, who had no money in their account but God mysteriously provided for all their needs? What about the stories we've heard or experienced of people who were ill and God healed them?

Setting our minds on these testimonies, reminding ourselves of the goodness of God, we are thinking about things that are pure, lovely, commendable, excellent, and worthy of praise. That's what we fill our minds with.

### 4. What is good?

We also need to keep going back to the scriptures about living in community with one another so that we can be encouraged. What are some scriptures you know by heart or can find about living in community?

### 5. What is helpful and beneficial?

One of the toughest things to do when I'm filled with depression and anxiety, is think about things that are actually helpful and beneficial, because I'm so bent to focus on everything that's messed up.

## TRAGEDY TO TRUTH

We love our worry. We don't know how to function without it. But, when we give things over to God, we've got to replace our thinking. Our thinking is different when we think about things that are true. For example: Ladies, look in the mirror. Most of you have an amplified, negative vision of how you really appear. So, you need to start listening to your husband. I don't mean asking questions like, "Do these pants make me look big?" That's a trap. We all know that. Rather, listen to your husband saying, "You are my standard of beauty. You are most beautiful. You are lovely. You are a blessing. Even when we're old and saggy one day, you're going to be my hottie."

And guys, we often find our worth in our income and what's in the bank, in our success, in our fruitfulness in work. When it doesn't satisfy, we turn to pornography, drugs, drunkenness, or buying things.

But for girls and guys, your worth is found in who you are in Christ. That's true. Think about things that are lovely, things that are commendable, excellent, and worthy of praise. When we're anxious, we tend to turn to things that are broken and destructive. We dwell on old relationships that we think would be better than the one we're in. We think about the false saviors we try to fill up our hearts with, and it just creates more worry.

In verse 9, Paul encourages us to practice what we have heard and learned and received. **What will you do the next time worry threatens to overtake you? Write it out here:**

CHAPTER 13

# A FIELD OF BROKEN WELLS

*". . . and the peace of God will be with you."*

Be appalled, O heavens, at this;
    be shocked, be utterly desolate,
declares the LORD,
    <sup>13</sup> for my people have committed two evils:
they have forsaken me,
    the fountain of living waters,
and hewed out cisterns for themselves,
    broken cisterns that can hold no water.

— Jeremiah 2:12-13 (ESV)

The prophet Jeremiah brought this charge against God's people because they had turned away from God, the source of life and their living water. Instead they went and dug wells that looked as if they could sustain life, but they were leaky and ultimately led to death.

I confess to you, I have relied upon many things in my life to make me whole, to give me a sense of value and purpose. I've relied upon popularity, girls, stuff, friends, approval of others, alcohol, and even religion to try to find some meaning in life. But none of those things worked, and they didn't work because they **couldn't** work; they were **never going to** work.

They were broken wells, incapable of holding water, much less giving me any shot at the life I was created to live.

They left me wanting more, and if I'd stayed with those things as my ultimate hope, then I would have ended up dead, not just physically but spiritually as well.

You see, that's the problem with broken wells. At first they seem like they are working and are life-giving wells. But the more you rely upon them to sustain your life, the more you realize they will leave you for dead.

I know I'm totally speaking in a figurative sense right now, talking about broken wells that don't hold water, so let me break it down in real life terms.

## MY OWN BROKEN WELLS

As a teenager, I couldn't wait for my parents to take a day-trip down to the coast for seafood. It gave me the opportunity to have my girlfriend over to fool around, to look at pornography, or to drink deeply of the other forbidden sins that I had come to love so much. My physical craving for excitement; the lust, and passion that rose up inside me, those things I could satisfy, at least temporarily.

## A FIELD OF BROKEN WELLS

But though I was physically satisfied, I was spiritually thirsty…Oh, so thirsty.

I desperately needed God to quench my thirst, but instead I looked for love, satisfaction and joy through created things. Everything God made, He made to draw us to Him with a sense of gratitude. But I had taken those things He created and made them my gods. They seemed life-giving, fulfilling my immediate needs, but they constantly left me thirsty and ultimately headed towards death.

## RUNNING TO EMPTY WELLS

Let me explain it this way.

Your attention, affection, and allegiance are all key for worshipping. If you are valuing anything higher than God's work through Jesus Christ by the power of the Holy Spirit, then you are worshipping something else. You are giving your attention, affection, and allegiance to something or someone else. You are running towards an empty well. It holds no value for you, despite what it **feels** like.

We trust what it **feels like**, and that is the deception.

I know how it is, especially for those who grew up in the church. You have the right Sunday School answers, and on paper you are running towards Jesus. But, between the two of us (and Jesus), you are likely not running full-tilt towards Him. You are running towards a broken well. They look good, sound good, and even smell good, but there is that pesky leak at the bottom that will eventually win, and leave the well, and you, dry.

Unfortunately, instead of abandoning these things we know are killing us (physically and spiritually), instead of abandoning these leaky wells, we try to plug the leaks.

How do we do that? **By justifying our sin.**

TRAGEDY TO TRUTH

Here's what I mean by that.

Anytime someone confronts us with our sin (our leaky wells), we immediately go on full alert to try to block for them. We justify them, downgrade them, dismiss them, or ignore them altogether.

We might be able to fool ourselves and maybe even those around us, but at the end of the day we're sipping on a fancy-looking but very leaky and contaminated well. It will kill us if we do not run away and run towards the Living Water.

It will leave us spiritually dead.

# WHAT IS SPIRITUAL DEATH ANYWAY AND WHY DOES IT MATTER?

I have come to realize that the first part of my life was filled with the work of creating better looking but still broken wells. Even though I have now been connected to the source of life through Jesus, I am still tempted to craft my own life-giving death traps, broken wells. I am still inclined to go after things that were given as a blessing and make them the ultimate. We all are. And that is called sin.

The Bible says in Ephesians 2:1-3,

And you were dead in the trespasses and sins in which you once walked, following the course of this world, following the prince of the power of the air, the spirit that is now at work in the sons of disobedience—among whom we all once lived in the passions of our flesh, carrying out the desires of the body and the mind, and were by nature children of wrath, like the rest of mankind.

## A FIELD OF BROKEN WELLS

Sin is anything that misses the mark of perfection that God is. It's the point when we take our lives in our own hands and ignore the One who made us.

We all do it.

We all sin. And we like it.

We all go after the broken wells.

But sin, if we stay there, leaves us spiritually dead, eternally separated from God.

# RELIGION IS A BROKEN WELL

For me, I think I often thought I was okay because I was religious. But now I know that religion only complicates things. I'm not talking about following Jesus, I'm talking about religion; there's a difference. The difference between religion and following Jesus may appear subtle, but it is imperative to understand it.

With religion, it is about you. It's about your performance, your ability, keeping the rules, and being as close to perfect as possible. Following Jesus is about understanding that, on your best day, you are not perfect enough. Even if you desire to be perfect, your heart is bent away from God and towards stuff that was made by God. Your drive is to become your own God, an impossible and deadly dream.

Jesus, however, was perfect and could and did live a perfect life. By living that way, He made a way for all of us broken people to be made right with God. He died a sacrificial death that we all deserve, a death that was not only physically brutal, but also spiritually devastating. He became sin on our behalf, so that by trusting in Him we could be made right with God (2 Corinthians 5:21). He is **the only way** that we can be connected to the source of life, to the Living Water.

The good news is that Jesus gives us living water (John 4:13-15). This water is completely different than the water in

**101**

the broken wells because it doesn't cause death. Instead, it gives life. The life it gives is continual, lasting, and consequential.

# JESUS, THE WELL OF LIFE

We can be confident in His ability to give life, bring transformation, and continue working in us, because whatever Jesus begins, Jesus finishes (Philippians 1:6).

**The first step** is realizing and accepting the fact that we are in constant need of the grace of Jesus. Fortunately, He is able and willing to provide unlimited grace. Jesus doesn't start a good work and then leave it to us to do the rest on our own. Nor does He give up and walk away from something He begins. If He begins it, He finishes it. If He saves us, He keeps us, restores us, and transforms us.

This is so important to remember when we find ourselves drifting back towards the broken wells, because we will drift back. It is a constant struggle, and there will always be appealing idols to draw our attention and affection. Jesus is the source of life, and anything we make supreme over Him will ultimately lead us to our death. We must be aware of this in order to move forward in our walk with Jesus.

The Gospel of Jesus Christ is about what God accomplished in spite of us. It is about God providing life to those who were dead. It is about God, the living water, being the very source of life. Not a source, but THE source. We are prone to run towards other things that seem easier and more accessible to give us life when, in reality, God has already made the only way available to all who will call on the name of Jesus.

Jesus is our life-giving well. I like how Mother Theresa put it. She said, "Every day I dip my bucket and drink deeply from the well that is Jesus."

**A FIELD OF BROKEN WELLS**

# DISCUSSION QUESTIONS

1. Have you ever found yourself feeling dissatisfied by things you built your life around? What were those "broken wells?"

2. If you discover that you have been trusting in something other than God to make your life complete, will it be difficult for you to repent and put that thing below God? Why or why not?

3. In this chapter, the statement was made that "your drive is to become your own God, an impossible and deadly dream." Do you agree or disagree with this view of our sinfulness? Can you support your answer with Scripture?

4. In light of the hope we have to find true satisfaction in Christ, how will you live differently?

CHAPTER 14

# GIRLS

I've always liked girls. From a young age, I remember thinking girls were pretty and enjoying how they smelled. Even though I liked girls, I was very shy around them and froze up if one came near me and started talking to me, especially around girls who were not in my family.

I can remember the name of my first crush in Kindergarten. I know that's weird, but it's true. Her name was Jennifer and she had brown hair, big brown eyes, and freckles. I'm not sure if I ever actually spoke to her, but I know I stared at her for a long time and daydreamed about talking to her and playing on the playground together. I had a vivid imagination.

A vivid imagination is not bad in itself, but it became my playground for sin, especially where girls were concerned.

## AN IDLE MIND

There is a saying that goes, "an idle mind is the devil's playground." I wouldn't say my mind was ever idle. In fact, I'd say it was always active. But nonetheless my active imagination also seemed to be the devil's playground.

## TRAGEDY TO TRUTH

I only had to think about something once or see it briefly for it to get set up on instant replay in my imagination. Once there, those thoughts cycled through my mind over and over and over.

My first exposure to pornography was at a very young age and occurred after my family got cable television. One night, as I was flipping through the channels on the TV, I came across a channel that was not like any other channel I had seen before. There were people on it who were wearing no clothes and were doing things that I never imagined people would do. I quickly changed the channel, because I knew instinctively that I shouldn't have watched it.

For the next few years I'd occasionally come across that channel and see things that made me feel both excited and disgusted. And as the pictures of what I'd seen replayed in my mind, I felt guilty and ashamed, a fact that made it very uncomfortable to be around girls at times.

But fast forward just a few years down the road, and I was actively finding ways to watch the forbidden channel. One day, I was flipping through the channels in my parent's room, keeping one eye on the television and one eye on the door. (I had become really good at hitting the 'Last Channel' button, so if my parents ever walked in, I was able to change the channel quickly.)

On that particular day, something went wrong with the remote. When my mom walked in the room, instead of changing the channel, I pushed the wrong button. But it was too late. She saw what I saw, and she screamed. I was terrified of what was going to happen and I ran up to my bathroom and locked the door. I screamed, "Mom, I'm ready for 'the talk' now!"

Her response was, "I'LL GIVE YOU A TALK!"

I'm not sure how I avoided getting punished, but I remember my mom, whom I was very close to, went to her

106

bathroom, and I could hear her weeping from upstairs. She was devastated, and I was very scared.

As I recall, my dad didn't say too much during all of this, but once she calmed down, my mom called me downstairs and gave me "the talk." To say it was awkward is a profound understatement. I was so embarrassed and sad that my mom caught me watching pornography.

I wish I could say that I never looked at pornography again, but unfortunately I'd still sneak away when I could to find that channel again. To make matters worse, since I had such a vivid imagination, I didn't have to see much in order to have a lot to fantasize about. As I neared Middle School, those thoughts increasingly consumed my mind and definitely had an effect on how I viewed women.

Keep in mind, I wasn't even in middle school yet.

# THE WRONG IDEA

While I was scared of girls and wasn't yet at a place where I wanted to do what I saw, I no longer just looked at girls as the prettier of the genders. They had become objects that I would one day use. As I started to go out with girls, I didn't judge them based upon their personality as much as I did upon their bodies. I know this is not uncommon for pre-adolescent boys, but there was a deep and creeping perversion forming because of my exposure to pornography.

I often joke about my middle school and high school relationships, but there was a clear progression from innocence to brokenness during middle school. By the end of middle school, I was becoming a predator rather than a boy just enjoying the company of a lady. I know some might think this is harsh for me to say about myself because our culture so openly accepts this type of behavior and dismisses it as "boys will be boys." *To be clear, I don't mean predator as in stalking and hurting women. I mean I had formed the wrong idea in my mind as to what their purpose was on this earth; namely to bring me physical and emotional satisfaction.

Fortunately for me, the Internet had not yet been created for public use, so it was difficult to find places to get pornography. Yet, I was still able to find it from time to time and enjoyed looking at it whenever I could. As I finished Middle School, my perversion moved from an intellectual obsession to a drive to act on those feelings.

# FINDING FREEDOM

At the beginning of high school, I began to act on my desires with girls. I went through a season of not really caring about them, who they were, what they were interested in, or even their feelings. I began to focus more on what I could get them to do with me. The odd thing is that I was not really interested in having intercourse, because someone close to our family was diagnosed with HIV, and I was scared of getting sick or getting a girl pregnant. However, as high school progressed, I began to lower my standards on that issue as well.

I could say more about how my sexual activity progressed, but I won't, because it is not my desire to glorify my behavior as something that should be emulated. However, I feel it is important to share how the pervasive nature of sexuality and pornography negatively affected my view of girls and how I interacted with them.

My sexual sin and enjoyment of pornography didn't stop after I became a Christian. In fact, for a while, I justified my behavior as something that "everyone does." The problem with this philosophy, the "everyone does it" excuse, is that I based the "rightness" of my sexual behavior on what my friends

## GIRLS

thought was okay (and did) instead of what I knew God communicated.

During my college years, a few years after I became a Christian, I was wrestling with the appropriateness of looking at pornography. Because I was growing as a Christian, I began to feel guilty about looking at images of random women doing random things with random people.

Finally, I was convinced that looking at pornography was not honoring to God and was not honoring to my fiancé. As I turned this corner, I began searching the Scriptures to find passages that communicated truths that would help me find freedom from pornography and sexual sin.

The Lord, in His kindness, brought my attention to Galatians 5:24. It says, "And those who belong to Christ Jesus have crucified the flesh with its passions and desires."

This passage landed on me with great weight. I sensed God's Spirit telling me, "You don't have to any longer. It's been put to death with Jesus."

By God's grace, my heart and mind changed about pornography, and from that point forward I thought differently about it and do not consume it any longer. Being set free from my need for pornography was incredible, but my view of women had been heavily tarnished by that point. I'm not blaming women for my need for pornography, I'm blaming pornography for the way I viewed women.

Over time, God has helped me to view women as valued, equal creations who are made by God, for God. The Golden Rule in Matthew 7:12 states, "So whatever you wish that others would do to you, do also to them, for this is the Law and the Prophets." This isn't just a general statement. It specifically applies to all aspects of our lives, even our interaction with the opposite sex.

Since I have been married, and especially after we began having children, my view of girls and women has been purified.

# TRAGEDY TO TRUTH

In His grace, God has helped me to value and cherish my wife, love and desire to protect my daughters, and view other women as sisters and nothing more. This is not to say that temptation doesn't occur, but as God continues to work on me and in me, I experience His freedom.

Marital intimacy is a huge gift given by God for the purpose of procreation and pleasure in the covenant of marriage. It is a gift to be enjoyed frequently and is not sinful or dirty in marriage. These truths need to be taught to teenagers, especially as they become aware of their own sexual desires. The way to help people through these struggles isn't shame and guilt. We can help them through vision, direction, and sharing the hope that we have through a relationship with Jesus Christ.

---

62% of boys have had their first exposure to pornography by the age of 11

82% of all first time accidental exposure to porn happens in the home of the child[ii]

75% of all children under the age of 18 have seen pornography

52% of boys and 47% of teenage high school girls admit some form of addiction to pornography

1 in 5 teenagers have posted nude or semi-nude pictures of themselves online

www.enoughisenough.org

---

[ii] *www.enoughisenough.org*

**GIRLS**

# DISCUSSION QUESTIONS

1. Our relationship with Christ should define our relationships with others. Do you feel like this is true for you? Why or why not?

2. Have you ever been in a relationship with another person, not just romantically, in which you felt a greater need for them than you do for God? What are the signs?

3. Sexual sin can be uniquely painful. If you have experienced this pain, you understand. 1 John 1:7 says, "But if we walk in the light, as [God] is in the light, we have fellowship with one another, and the blood of Jesus his Son cleanses us from all sin." How does the word "all" change how you feel about your sexual sin?

4. Once we put faith in Jesus, what does our primary goal become in our relationships towards the opposite sex?

5. What are you looking for in a potential husband or wife? Do you think it is wrong to hold your future spouse to a higher standard than you have lived up to in regards to sexual sin?

CHAPTER 15

# TEMPTATION

Temptation is the desire to act out in a way that we know is against God's Word. It might be doing something opposed to His Word or it might be avoiding something that is inline with His Word. Temptation, in and of itself is not a sin.

It is acting upon temptation that is the problem.

Early on as a Christian I frequently gave in to temptation, sinning and feeling guilty about both the temptation and the sin itself. As I grew in my relationship with Jesus, I realized there was a difference between temptation and sin. My sin became less enjoyable, so I began to make different choices. But, even though I was sinning less, it seemed like temptation continued to increase. The more I felt tempted to do something, the more I felt guilty, which is never productive, especially for someone prone to depression.

## AN INVITATION TO WORSHIP

Several years ago, I counseled a youngman who struggled with some pretty deeps in issues, mostly because of sins committed

# TRAGEDY TO TRUTH

against him. He shared how defeated he felt because he was tempted to return to his sin.

I finally stopped him and asked, "Have you acted on that temptation?" He said, "No way. I haven't acted on that temptation, but man, I just feel so defeated." I smiled at him, and I said, "Well, I'm excited for you."

He looked at me like I was a crazy person. "What do you mean you're excited? What I am telling you about is horrible." I said, "Look, I'm excited for you because temptation is an invitation to worship."

Here's what I meant. You'll either worship Satan by sinning when you're tempted, or you'll resist temptation and honor Jesus by obeying him. We need to start viewing temptation more as an opportunity to worship than something that defeats us.

If you're being tempted, then that's not necessarily a bad thing. That means you're becoming a threat. That means you are having influence. That means the enemy is concerned with slowing you down so you will have less impact for the sake of the kingdom and advancing the gospel.

Hebrews 2:18 says, *"For because he himself has suffered when tempted, he is able to help those who are being tempted."* Temptation is not a sin. Jesus Himself was tempted in all ways, yet without sin.

And in Hebrews 4:15, the writer of Hebrews says this, *"For we do not have a High Priest who is unable to sympathize with our weaknesses, but one who in every respect has been tempted as we are, yet without sin."*

We have a High Priest, Jesus, who understands what we are going through when we are tempted. He can say, "I've been there. I was tempted in every way, but I resisted." We don't have a High Priest who is espousing morality and an ideal that no one is able to live up to, but we have a High Priest who is proclaiming power and freedom from sin.

114

TEMPTATION

You don't have to sin any longer. If you do not act on the temptation, then you are not in sin. You have not offended God. You're not going against God's will if you resist the temptation. Martin Luther summed it up well when he said, "You can't stop a bird from landing on your head, but you can stop it from building a nest there."

# RESIST THE DEVIL AND DRAW NEAR

We're told in James 4:7 to resist the devil. Now, that doesn't mean put on literal armor, get superstitious, put up your dream catcher, and burn certain demon hindering incense.

When James tells us to "resist the devil" he's not warning us of a visible attack of a talking serpent or a red-horned cartoon character with a pitch fork.

Temptation is way more subtle than that. Something, either internal or external in our lives, brings us to a place where we simply don't want to obey God. The enemy uses our thoughts and circumstances to tempt us, to lie to us, to make us believe that God doesn't want what's best for us, but instead wants to keep us from doing and having all that we are entitled to.

James is telling us we have the power through Christ to resist temptation, to remove ourselves from temptation, and to push through the temptation.

But we also must do more than just "resist the devil." If we just resist the devil, we'll eventually lose because we are doing it on our own strength.

After resisting what he is tempting us to do, then we must draw near to God.

James 4:8 says, *"Draw near to God, and"* —here's a promise— *"he will draw near to you."*

When I'm feeling tempted, I ask God to help me. I ask Jesus for his power. I ask the Holy Spirit to guide me towards

# TRAGEDY TO TRUTH

what is right. That's worship. That's giving worth to God. Worship isn't just when you have the warm fuzzies and you're singing a song you like.

The Bible says that when we "draw near to God," God draws near to us. He doesn't abandon us. He doesn't leave us. He comes.

There are times when you may not sense that God is close, but He is. When you're able to overcome the temptation and not give into sin, it's an opportunity to rejoice in the freedom that God has given you through his Son, Jesus. "Resist the devil," and "draw near to God."

As we draw near to God, He draws near to us and we have an opportunity to be victorious over temptation and sin and to cultivate deeper intimacy with Him.

Even as we draw near to God, satan can still use temptation against us.

"But God, I'm being tempted. I'm so filthy with that temptation."

In Matthew 11:28-30 the author records Jesus saying, *"Come to me, all who labor and are heavy laden, and I will give you rest. Take my yoke upon you, and learn from me, for I am gentle and lowly in heart, and you will find rest for your souls. For my yoke is easy, and my burden is light."*

Jesus is saying, "Hey, come to me when you're jacked up. Don't run away and go into that sin. Your temptation hasn't made you filthy, even if your temptation is filthy."

We draw near to God, and God draws near to us. It cultivates intimacy. If you're only going to God when you've been good and having good and whole some thoughts, then you don't really know God. Knowing God is going to Him with your filth and your brokenness and the propensity and bent we have towards sin and saying, "God, do you love me still?" And, His answer is always a resounding, "Yes, I do," and

116

## TEMPTATION

He'll graciously remind you that He is better than anything that you can be tempted to do or not do.

# PROTECTING YOURSELF FROM GIVING IN TO TEMPTATION

### 1. Know the Word

The easiest way to get close to anyone is to spend time with them. We spend time with God by praying, by sitting in His presence, and by reading His Word. Simply put, you need to know the Word. Why? It's easy for us to say, "Well, Jesus didn't sin because He was God."

We kind of give up right there. If He was just God and not human then that would make sense, but He was also fully man. Because He was fully man, He had to rely on His father through the Word, just like we do.

In Matthew 4:1-11 Jesus faced temptation. He didn't just go and lay down or say, "I'm God; therefore, it doesn't bother me." No, He had to know the Word in order to use it to resist the devil, to draw near to God, and also to identify when Satan, who knows the Bible very well, was distorting the truth.

Satan used scripture to try to help Jesus justify sin. He tried to use God's own words to convince Jesus of something that simply was not true.

But Jesus knew what was being said to Him was not biblical or accurate, so He responded, "It is written." He submitted to the written Word of God, which He had committed to memory.

He did not trust His emotions or how he felt (keep in mind he had to have been incredibly weak when he was in the desert with the enemy because he hadn't eaten in 40 days!).

I don't know about you, but my emotions betray me daily. If I allowed my emotions to dictate where I go, what I do, and

**117**

TRAGEDY TO TRUTH

why I do it, then I would be a very different person. Even Jesus, at a point of weakness after not eating for forty days, did not rely on his own strength to overcome temptation when he was tempted by the devil." He relied upon the Word of God.

## 2. Look for an Exit Sign

Another way we deal with temptation is by looking for an exit sign.

In 1 Corinthians 10:13 it says, "*No temptation has overtaken you that is not common to man. God is faithful, and he will not let you be tempted beyond your ability, but with the temptation he will also provide the way of escape, that you may be able to endure it.*"

Paul is reminding the people of Corinth that there is always going to be a way out. God is never going to allow you to be tempted beyond what He knows you are able to bear, especially with His help. He'll always provide a way out, a way forward, a way of rescue. He's a rescuing God.

There's always going to be a way out. There will always be an off button. There will always be a door. There will always be a vehicle. There are other friends you can make if you need to. There will always be an apology. Sometimes the way out is to apologize. Look for the exit signs.

## 3. Recognize that Temptation Helps You Grow

God is not a cruel, sadistic God who wants to see you get hurt and see how bad you can be messed up. He will never allow you to go beyond what you can handle. It's like a good weight trainer. When I work out there are times where I'm on number seven and tell my spotter, "I'm good," and he says, "No, you've got two more in you." At first, I'm thinking, "You're just crazy and like to watch me shake." But he knows the way I work, the

# TEMPTATION

way I lift. He knows how the body works, and he never allows me to go to the point of injury. I have never been injured, even though I continue to lift heavier and heavier weights.

In the same way, the Lord wants you to grow. You have to be pushed a little so you have the opportunity to grow. That's why God allows you to be tempted. If you're always in a place where there's no temptation, you're not growing in your worship, in your ability to draw near to God, and in your understanding of the Word of God.

## 4. Know Yourself

It's not whether you're being tempted; it's what you do with it. Part of knowing the Word and resisting the devil is knowing yourself. For instance, if you know that you struggle with your weight, then an all you can eat buffet may not be the best place to go. Don't be a jerk about it and say that no one should go to an all you can eat buffet, because some people don't have overeating problems.

You can't be a legalist towards everyone, "Well, no one can go, because I can't go." No, you're just bitter, not godly. It's like telling married people not to be together because their single friends will be jealous. Sure, you may not want to be overly romantic in front of your single friends. Just be discerning, and really know yourself.

# WHAT TO DO WHEN YOU DO GIVE IN TO TEMPTATION

When you fail (and you will), when you don't resist the devil, when you don't fight, when you don't trust the Word of God, and when you give in to sin, you need to run TO Jesus, not away from Him.

Many give in to temptation, and then they just turn their back on the entire faith. When you give in to temptation and when you're in sin, run to Jesus. He is able and willing to forgive you of your sin, to cleanse you of all unrighteousness, to make you right with the Father.

Christians are not forming a country club. We're not building a hall of fame for saints. We're not trying to build a community of perfect people. We're trying to say, "We're people who need Jesus." We fail at times. We need each other. We need to pray for each other, pray with each other, do battle together, and look out for each other, thanking God for every victory. We need to be a family that looks out for one another and serves one another.

1 John 9 says, "If we confess our sins, he is faithful and just to forgive us our sins and to cleanse us from all unrighteousness." Our sin no longer identifies us. Our sin no longer enslaves us. We are free from the consequence of sin, which is death. We are saved to life and righteousness. Our Lord gives life. The enemy brings death.

## DON'T LIVE IN FEAR

And lastly, don't live in fear of temptation and sin. When temptations arise, you can either choose to sin at the expense of honoring God, or you can resist, draw near to God, and God will draw near to you. You are worshiping Him, growing in intimacy and greater maturity in the faith.

Don't be afraid to get out there and live your life.

If you live in a bubble and you don't listen, watch, touch, eat, drink, or anything else, then that's not really victory. That's fear. We're not called to be scared of everything. We're called to live in freedom. Freedom is messy at times.

I'm not saying, "Well, go out and sin and God will forgive you anyways." I'm saying if we live hidden in our sub-Christian

## TEMPTATION

Culture all the time, we're not influencing the culture. We're not making disciples of Jesus. We're not helping the lost become found. We're hiding. And hiding in fear is not living.

As you go and make disciples, you'll come across temptation. One of my professors in seminary, Dr. Rodney Woo, put it this way. "Spiritual maturity isn't really gauged on how much you sin or don't sin. Spiritually maturity is gauged on the tie between sin and repentance."

As you grow in the Lord, you become more aware of your sin and you're able to repent and know that you're free. When you're being tempted, look at it as an opportunity to take it to Jesus and say, "Jesus, you already know what's going on in my brain. Help me in my unbelief." Call your friend. Call a prayer partner, "Hey, I'm really struggling with this. Will you pray for me?"

If you're in Christ, your sin doesn't separate you from God, but it also doesn't allow you to live in the freedom that Christ has purchased for you. As C. S. Lewis put it, you're settling for "mud pies" instead of the great feast. Overcome temptation through Christ and enjoy the feast.

## DISCUSSION QUESTIONS

1. If you are a Christian, has your desire to sin decreased since you put faith in Jesus? What evidence would you point to?

2. How is temptation different from sin?

3. Is it difficult for you to imagine that temptations play a necessary role in our Christian progress? Why or why not?

4. What temptations seem to hit you the hardest or seem to be most frequent? What can you do to build defenses against sinning as a result of these temptations?

## TRAGEDY TO TRUTH

5. Are you ashamed of your temptations? If so, why do you feel this way?

6. What hope do you take from knowing Jesus was tempted in every way we are?

CHAPTER 16

# HOPEFUL

For we are his workmanship,
    created in Christ Jesus for good works,
which God prepared beforehand,
    that we should walk in them.

— **Ephesians 2:10 (ESV)**

I once heard Dr. John Piper say, "I don't agree with where he has been, I am not sure of where he is, but I am hopeful for where he is going."[1] This is a helpful way to think about someone who has come to faith in Jesus. While their past may have been rough and their life is still a mess, we can rest assured that Jesus is at work and that He will bring the necessary change in His timing.

---

1   God has used the ministry of John Piper greatly in my life over the years. For more about John Piper go to http://www.DesiringGod.org.

For many years, the crash was the identifying marker on my life. While people slowly began to trust me as I was living differently and speaking a lot, I still felt like I was no good. As a young Christian, I had a hard time believing that God could love me after what I had done. No matter how much I spoke to students and was told that I was making a difference, I still had this feeling that I would always walk in the shadow of my former sin.

As I grew in my understanding of the Gospel over the years, I began to grasp the truth that I was no longer defined by my sin. Jesus actually paid for it all, the big and small, so that through Him I am made right with God. The Bible actually says in 2 Corinthians 5:21, "For our sake he made him to be sin who knew no sin, so that in him we might become the righteousness of God." This means that God made Jesus, who was without sin, to become sin as our substitute. His sacrifice on the cross was payment enough for us to become right with God if we trust Jesus.

# GOOD WORKS

The Apostle Paul writes in Ephesians 2:10 that we are God's 'workmanship', meaning that He is mindful not only of our creation, but also our redemption. When God saves someone through Jesus Christ, He makes him or her new, not just recycled.[2] He is mindful of us, He cares for us, and He loves us. We are His and He has plans for us that He has already laid out. Becoming a Christian isn't just about going to Heaven when we die. It is about following Jesus now and living the life He has planned for us.

---

2    See 2 Corinthians 5:17

HOPEFUL

I came to realize that although I had made horrible mistakes, God's grace is big enough to cover them and to forgive them. He rescued me from my sin in order to use me now to point other people to Jesus. From the time I realized this, I have been committed to this purpose. I was spared from much, in order to be used by God to do what He has laid out for me to do. Essentially, this is the essence of understanding God's will and following it.

Even though I was not perfect after I trusted Jesus, I was forgiven. This forgiveness gave me the freedom and the privilege of being able to know God and have a relationship with Him now. Not only was I able to have a relationship with Him but I was also able to point other people to Him through Jesus as well.

Now all that I do is focused through the lens of my desire to know God and to make Him known. My ultimate purpose is to live as His representative by introducing people to Jesus and inviting them to trust Him for the forgiveness of their sins and the promise of eternal life. This is the primary 'good works' God gives to all of those who follow Jesus.

# GOOD NEWS

My whole reason for writing this book is so that you will consider the Gospel of Jesus Christ. Gospel simply means 'good news'. The good news is that you were created by God to know God and to enjoy Him. However, we all have sinned against God and, as a consequence, we deserve punishment, both physical and spiritual. The Bible says in Ephesians 2:1-3 that we are dead in our sins and, consequently, targets for God's punishment for sin.

The good news is, although God would have been right in punishing us for our sins, He sent His own Son, Jesus Christ, to live the life we could not live on our own (Ephesians 2:4-9).

125

He lived a sinless life and then died a horrific death on the cross. While we should be the ones facing God's punishment for sin, Jesus took our place as our substitute so that all who believe in Him will not spend an eternity separated from God.

Every human being has messed up in one way or another. We all mess up in many ways throughout our lives. The hope we have is not that we will become better, but that Jesus is best and is able to help us. He is our hope for the future, both in this life and the next. It is my aim to make Jesus known at home, in my neighborhood, in my church, and to the world.

This isn't just because I'm a Pastor, but because I believe that Jesus redeems us so that we can be agents of redemption throughout our lives. When I first started speaking to students, it was partly motivated by my desire to give something back and to make a difference. Over time, my motivation became based upon the love God has for me and has shown for me through Jesus. I once had a mentor and friend say, "Jesus saved me, so I will live my life as a 'Thank You!'"

Once believers begin to realize that our lives are not being lived to pay God back, then we will begin to pursue the things that matter to God. In fact, the mere idea that we can pay God back is silly. It's like saying we are going to collect coins and pay back a multi-trillion dollar loan. It's impossible. We cannot pay God back for the enormous gift that He has given to us in Jesus Christ.

## STILL GROWING

In the summer of 2012, I had the privilege of going to Kenya. I spent ten days there preaching and teaching in a seminary. My time there was a great opportunity to see how Jesus is at work. In the midst of great poverty and brokenness, people are coming to faith in Jesus, and new churches are being planted.

**HOPEFUL**

There are impoverished Africans who are caring for those in equally dire situations. My heart was both broken and full of rejoicing at the same time. The hope that I have in the Gospel of Jesus Christ grew during my time there and I saw that we all have a part to play in making a difference in this world.

Since God has made such an impact on my life, I want to help pastors and teachers in Kenya make the same impact on others, and every dollar helps them reach more people. God has wired us with various gifts, and He redeems those gifts when He saves us through Jesus. We can be used by God to bring redemption to those around us in our immediate contexts as well as to those across the planet. Everyone who is in Christ has a purpose that God laid out before him or her, but the challenge is whether or not you will pursue that purpose.

## WHERE ARE YOU?

The question for you is: Where are you with Jesus? Do you know Him? Have you trusted Him? Perhaps you feel like you have been too bad, or have sinned too much. The great news is that God's grace is bigger than anything we have done and the love of Jesus is able to cover a multitude of sins (1 Peter 4:8). Jesus has made a way for you to be right with God the Father and you don't have to get cleaned up before you trust Him.

Or perhaps you are not convinced that you have a need for forgiveness. After all, you might be thinking, "Well, I'm not nearly as bad as Casey was," which is likely true. The important thing to realize is that I am not the standard of perfection, or in biblical terms, holiness. God is. The Bible states in Romans 3:21-26:

[21]But now the righteousness of God has been manifested apart from the law, although the Law and the Prophets bear witness to it— [22]the righteousness of God through faith in Jesus

## TRAGEDY TO TRUTH

Christ for all who believe. For there is no distinction: [23]for all have sinned and fall short of the glory of God, [24]and are justified by his grace as a gift, through the redemption that is in Christ Jesus, [25]whom God put forward as a propitiation by his blood, to be received by faith. This was to show God's righteousness, because in his divine forbearance he had passed over former sins. [26]It was to show his righteousness at the present time, so that he might be just and the justifier of the one who has faith in Jesus.

In this passage, we see that since humanity is unable to maintain the Law of the Old Testament, then God has made a way through His Son, Jesus Christ. Without Jesus, we all fall short of God's glory, and we cannot meet God's standard of perfection. Even the best human being is unable to do this. The only One who was able to do this was Jesus, and this is why He had to die to make final payment for those who would believe in Him.

My desire in writing this is not to sound preachy, but to continue to walk in the purposes that I was created and redeemed for through Jesus Christ. I want you to know Jesus and I want you to experience the great joy that I have in knowing Him and making Him known. While none of us are perfect, there is a Perfect One who is completely able and willing to wash us clean and make us new.

I am no hero, nor am I better than anyone else. I'm just a man who has sinned greatly and has been loved and forgiven of much. My desire is that you would trust Jesus to forgive you of your sins and make you right with God the Father. If you are already a follower of Jesus, then my prayer for you is that you will realize that your identity is in Jesus and not in what you have done, what you do, or what you will do. You have been created and redeemed for Him. Know Him, and as you know Him through His Word, the Bible, you will continue to grow in your understanding of the good deeds He has for you to walk in. Discover them and walk in them.

HOPEFUL

Have some fun along the way. We are not called to a life of drudgery as we love and follow Jesus. We are called to be bright lights and salty salt. We are called to make disciples as we go, and we are called to love God and our neighbors with all that we have. This is possible by the help of God, the Holy Spirit.

It is a joy to know that God is still unfolding our stories, and He is the best storyteller. My prayer for you is that you will trust Him to do His job as God and you will find great joy and rest in your response of loving obedience. As you live this life, let God form His story in you and through you. By doing so, you will know His love and grace, and you will be used mightily for His glory and for your great joy.

# DISCUSSION QUESTIONS

1. What sins do you still feel define who you are, even in part?

2. 1 Corinthians 5:17 says, "Therefore, if anyone is in Christ, he is a new creation. The old has passed away; behold, the new has come." What does this say about your former sins?

3. Tragedy to Truth is a story about hope in Christ when all seems lost. What tragedies are you hopeful to see God apply the truth of the gospel to?

4. When you imagine God redeeming some broken part of your past, do you feel scared or anxious about how that would look? Why or why not? What does the Bible say about your fears and anxieties?

5. Are you ever tempted to use good works or religion to pay God back? What truths do we need to remember when we feel this way?

# APPENDIX A—WHAT'S YOUR STORY?

The saying is trustworthy and deserving of full acceptance, that Christ Jesus came into the world to save sinners, of whom I am the foremost. But I received mercy for this reason, that in me, as the foremost, Jesus Christ might display his perfect patience as an example to those who were to believe in him for eternal life.

## 1 TIMOTHY 1:15–16

Every Christian has a story to tell of how God rescued them from sin and death, into life and righteousness through Jesus Christ. As we see in these verses, the Apostle Paul understood that God's redemptive work in him through Jesus Christ was not only so that he might be saved from his sin and placed into a right relationship with God, but also, it might serve as an illustration to those who do not yet believe.

## GOD'S STORY THROUGH OUR STORIES

Often times people have not thought through their story enough to be able to articulate it in a manner that conveys their need for rescue and forgiveness, and God's sent solution through Jesus Christ. Instead, it either becomes a glorification of their former sin or a boastful tirade of who they worked hard to become. Both instances are in error: they put us at the center of the story instead of God, since our stories are a part of God's bigger story.

One of the most helpful exercises I was ever encouraged to do was by one of my mentors when he challenged me to tell my story in three minutes or less. To be honest, I have an intense story, so condensing it down into three minutes, while including the redemption that occurred through Christ was challenging. However, it forced me to focus on what was most important in my story by being able to illustrate what was most important in God's story, which is God's grace to us through Jesus Christ.

## THE POINT OF THE STORY IS JESUS

I'd encourage you to take some time and think through how your story is a part of a larger story. It is God's story. Perhaps you grew up in a faithful Christian home and came to faith at a young age, then boast in God's grace and how you, a sinner, didn't deserve any of what he gave you. Maybe you were a religious kid who grew up knowing all of the "right" answers, but your heart was far from God. Maybe you didn't grow up in a Christian family. In any case, discuss how your sin and depravity was ultimately and completely redeemed through Jesus Christ, and how this salvation and redemption continues to be applied even today. Regardless of where you were prior to Christ, the point is that Jesus doesn't just make us better—he makes us new! (See 2 Corinthians 5:17.)

APPENDIX A—WHAT'S YOUR STORY?

# 6 TIPS WHEN TELLING YOUR STORY

Be honest about where you were, where you are, and where you sense Jesus is leading you. Here are a few things to think about as you work to craft your story in a helpful way:

**Who were you before you met Jesus?**

For some, this is an easy question to answer, for others, it is a revealing question. Don't try to make it more or less than it is, just be honest about who you were without Jesus.

**How did you first hear of Jesus?**

Was it a family member, friend, pamphlet, etc.? What was your initial response? Did you believe the first time you heard?

**What was your conversion like?**

Was it sudden, gradual, substantial, or simple? How did it feel? How was it applied (i.e. were there immediate changes, or gradual changes)?

**What is the most important thing you have learned about Jesus since your conversion?**

This is important, and may not be only one thing, but it might be helpful to have one theme going throughout your story when you prepare to share it with others. Was he your Redeemer? If so, what did he redeem you from?

**How has your view of yourself changed in view of your relationship with Jesus?**

What lies did you believe about yourself before you met Jesus? What truth has replaced those lies?

## TRAGEDY TO TRUTH

**How does your story best point people to Jesus?**

Is it a story of a criminal being forgiven of a crime? Is it one who was dead because of their sin finding life? Is it a story about someone being lost, then being found? Sound familiar? There are stories like this all over the Bible. There are stories like this being written today. You are a part of God's story!

The aim of our stories is ultimately to point people to Jesus. Our stories are not to tell people how great we are now—they're sober realizations of who we were without Christ and a hopeful presentation of who we hope to become in him. What is your story? Think through it, organize it, and then share it often.

# ACKNOWLEDGEMENTS

I want to thank Jesus Christ, my Lord and my Savior for rescuing me and for using me as a part of your Kingdom work.

I want to thank my dear wife Steph and our beautiful daughters Braelyn and Abigail for letting daddy take time to work on this project.

I want to thank my Mom, Carolyn, and my Dad, Allan, for standing by me and believing in me.

I want to thank my sister Alicia, her husband Jason, and her boys Noah and Jonah.

I want to thank Steve and Becky Jett for allowing me to marry their daughter and for being amazing in-laws!

I want to thank Tyler & Kelley Jett.

I want to thank the church I have the privilege of pastoring, Christ Community Church of Magnolia for supporting my family and I and for being a living representation of the Body of Christ.

## TRAGEDY TO TRUTH

I want to thank Carol Jones for working with me on this second edition to help me tell my story in a more clear and concise manner. Your help is invaluable to me, and the readers!

I want to thank Marissa Torres, the Project Manager at Lucid Books, you helped this project to completion.

I want to thank Rod & Diana Brace who have for many years, loved and cared for my family. We are so grateful for all that you have done, and more importantly for whom you are. We love you!

I want to thank the Board of Directors of Transform Ministries, as they have been a huge support along the way providing the love and accountability necessary for this ministry to flourish over the years.

I want to thank Ryan and Mike of Modern Trade – www.themoderntrade.com for donating the video to my Kickstarter campaign.

I want to thank Justin & Brandi Hyde for their years of friendship and support.

I want to thank Jason & Jennifer George for their ongoing friendship and support.

I want to thank Marty Nicolaus for reaching out to me after the crash and for taking a risk on me by letting me serve on his staff at Sugar Land FUMC.

I want to thank Micah Nicolaus for seeing something more inme than just a good story. Thanks for always encouraging me to see the Lord's work in my life beyond the crash.

## ACKNOWLEDGEMENTS

I want to thank Jeff McDowell for all of the talks and patience you showed me early in my walk with Jesus. You were an instrumental part.

I want to thank John & Linda Haskew for their years of friendship and support. Linda you were the perfect boss for me at the perfect time as I started my ministry.

I want to thank Chuck Land for your years of investment, mentoring, and coaching. I am grateful that you cared more about the man than just the ministry of the man.

I want to thank Tim Barosh for your friendship and years of encouragement and support.

I want to thank Joel Engle for the years of mentoring me. I learned so much from you and am grateful for our ongoing friendship.

I want to thank Kyle & Robin Byrd and Frontline Ministries for giving me a shot at their camps. These were the first camps I was asked to speak at and I learned so much from you both. Thank you.

I want to thank John & Kelly Sherrill and the 220 Family. You all have been a constant prayer support and great friends over the years.

I want to thank the people of Sugar Land FUMC, Crossbridge Church, and Redeemer Church Brenham, as you all were an amazing church family and had profound impact on who I am today. You all have always been so loving and supportive of Steph and I, and we are grateful.

## TRAGEDY TO TRUTH

I want to thank my brothers in the Acts 29 Church Planting Network for your friendship and support over the years. I'm grateful to be a part of such a great Kingdom work.

I want to thank the following people for their generous support in my Kickstarter Campaign: Justin & Brandi Hyde, Jason & Jennifer Pigott, Mike & Catherine Haskew, Dianne and Griff Evans, Robert and Julie Gau, John & Kelly Sherrill, Tony & Crystal Carbone, Jared and Robin Brient, Steve & Becky Jett, Mr. & Mrs. John K. Mickelson, Andrew James, Megan Porter, Steve & Jane Taylor, The Elms Family, Lee, Sarah, Joshua & Betsy Parker, Dean & Susan Johnson, Mark Cornett and McKinney Whetstone Cornett, Patrick & Jennifer Haskew, Kyle and Lisa Jantzen, Jason & Julie Clarke, Cornelius J. Ukena, Mark & Christine Meeker & Family, Bradley & Jessica Bevers, Zach, Candice & Conlin McNair, Alex & Tonya Leiva, Rhonda & Bruce Cease, Robert & Beth Panter, Robert & Michelle Copeland, and John Mattox.

# ABOUT THE AUTHOR

**Casey Cease** is the Lead Pastor of Christ Community Church of Magnolia and the Executive Director of Transform Ministries. He is married to his high school sweetheart, Stephanie, and has two daughters, Braelyn and Abigail. He travels frequently sharing the love of God through the message of Jesus Christ.

You can connect with Casey at the following places online:

www.caseycease.com
www.tragedytotruth.com
www.twitter.com/caseycease

CPSIA information can be obtained
at www.ICGtesting.com
Printed in the USA
LVOW08s0429220317
527936LV00001B/4/P